THE LEADERSHIP CONVERSATION

Make bold change,
one conversation at a time

Rose Fass

www.TotalPublishingAndMedia.com

Table of Contents

Dedication

For my Mom, Tess
May 14, 1924—May 10, 2020

Over the years, I have been invited to speak to many diverse audiences on the subject of leadership. Following these engagements, I am often asked if I have written a book. For those of you who have resonated with me, your encouragement inspired me to write my first book. *The Chocolate Conversation.* The 2020 Global Pandemic was the impetus for writing my second book *The Leadership Conversation.* I began writing it in the middle of the lockdown and as I found out, Shakespeare wrote King Lear and Isaac Newton developed calculus and discovered gravity, both while in quarantine!

I dedicate this book to my mom whose wisdom, strength and resilience taught me what it means to endure and stay calm in the midst of chaos. During the writing of my first book my father, a World War II Marine, a poet, and a business executive, fought his final battle. He died of congestive heart failure on Saturday August 18, 2012. Eight years later, while writing this book, mom passed four days shy of her 96th birthday, the morning of Mother's Day, May 10, 2020. This book is for you, Mom. Thank you for all the conversations that got me through life.

Some of the most important conversations are
the ones you have with yourself...

Thank you!

Many thanks to Heather Hummel Gallagher for the countless hours spent with me researching, fact checking, and editing this book. I miss our time together. Could not have gotten through it without you!

Foreword

Throughout my career, I tend to cautiously adopt wisdom from others. Too many "thought leaders" offer clever but unproven advice. Rose Fass, however, is a precious exception, with guidance that comes from a career's worth of success.

Rose and I first worked together when she participated in hiring me at Xerox, where she established herself as a mentor and a trusted counselor to many leaders. There she positively influenced many lives, including my own. Seventeen years after we first met, I hired her to join me at Gartner. A strategic thinker with a rare gift for bringing structure to chaos, Rose has consistently helped teams overcome their differences and collaborate to achieve amazing things. Her secret, which she reveals in *The Chocolate Conversation*, brings to mind something Henry Kissinger once told me—advice I have never forgotten: "Whatever must be done eventually should be done immediately." Rose understands something too many leaders easily forget; big bold change happens one conversation at a time, but without urgency and clarity, those critical conversations fall flat, and the whole organization suffers.

Rose's message is critical for these times. As the consumer revolution and rapid innovations in technology continue to disrupt entire industries, enterprises from New York to New Delhi are realizing constant change is a necessity. My advice to them and to you is to read this book. It will help you break through the inevitable chaos and more quickly drive success.

— Bill McDermott

Testimonial

If you are brave enough to suit up every morning, march on to the field and lean into the challenges of 'the game', you know one thing for sure, you're gonna get hurt! Well, welcome to leadership. In the words of Rose Fass, "leadership is messy. It's uncomfortable, exhilarating, and challenging. But let's face it, you wouldn't want it any other way. Like every great athlete, truly great leaders prepare, practice, learn, and possess two things: a plan and a coach.

This is where Rose comes in! If you are someone who hates the cheap seats, loves the game and gets up after every play...don't go on the field without her. Here's why.

People in the cheap seats talk about high level strategies and opine on 'what to do' while producing countless PowerPoints that are neither powerful nor 'to the point'. If this is you, enjoy the view and put this book down!

I've been working with Rose and the *fassforward* team for over 18 years. If you want to change the conversation, lead through the tough plays and build something truly special—don't go on the field without this playbook!

— Martha Delehanty, Chief People Officer,
Commvault & former CHRO, Verizon Business

Chapter One

A 50 Year Conversation

Childhood Lessons

I look back on my career now, and I see where and how the lessons of my childhood, and those of my early career in the corporate world, lead me to where I am today—talking to you. Some of the most important lessons didn't look like lessons at the time, they just looked like life.

I always gravitated to being a serial entrepreneur, even long before my leadership roles in large corporations. I inherited it from my dad, who went from being a WWII Marine to an appliance sales guy for Sears Roebuck and driving a clothing cleaners delivery truck on Saturdays, all while attending university at night on the GI bill.

As a kid, I often rode in the truck with him. After he dropped off cleaning to current customers, he would stop at homes in the neighborhood and pitch new business. Which by the way, on a weekly average, brought in two to three new customers.

I loved hearing my dad pitch the benefits of switching to the cleaners he represented. Having a cute little girl next to him added to the appeal. I would smile sweetly, look up at him adoringly and thank the moms for listening. We made a great team!

Returning to the truck, dad would fill in his new customer cards and I would stack them by street address. I loved being what was often referred to in the sales business as the "B" guy, or sales associate today. In this case I was the "B" girl.

We often chatted on those *ride-alongs* about different approaches to bringing in new customers. He took some of my ideas to heart. That made one young girl feel very special.

After Dad successfully graduated from university, he was promoted to Sales Manager at Sears. The increase in income allowed him to give up his Saturday job with the cleaners. It also meant moving away from Utica, New York where the entire family was born and raised. The extended families of both my parents lived in Utica, and here we were moving 65 miles down the throughway to Amsterdam, New York, a small upstate town. In Mom's eyes, we may as well have been moving to the other side of the country. She was totally bummed, even though my dad did all he could to convince her that while 65 miles was a bit of a drive, he would happily bring her home to visit family every weekend, if needed. She was inconsolable until dad drove us to Amsterdam for a *look-see.*

We went from exit 31 to exit 27 with the same radio station playing most of the way. Dad's way of subtly showing mom we were still in the vicinity.

Once we exited, Dad drove up Guy Park Avenue, which was tree lined and populated with old estates. My older brother and I had window seats in the back of dad's rambler with our baby brother wedged in the middle. We stared out the window with our mouths open. You see, we lived on an urban street in East Utica in a four flat home with a yard the size of a postage stamp.

Dad turned off Guy Park Avenue onto Van Dyke Avenue, which later became Golf Course Road. The golf course ran the length of the road on one side with lovely newly built homes on the other.

We pulled into the drive of a gorgeous blush colored 1950's multi-level home. Mom gasped and asked, *"Are we visiting your new boss?"* Dad said no. Mom then asked who he knew who lived in this beautiful home?

Dad paused, looked lovingly at my mom and said, *"My beautiful wife and her children, with me I hope."* What followed was a tearful incredulous reaction from my mom, *"Oh Peter, can we afford this?"* My brothers and I were already out of the car screaming with excitement waiting impatiently at our new front door. The inside did not disappoint. This house was a mansion to us. Every room was beautiful. Mom was *goo-gah* over having a powder room off the front entrance, and a private bath off the master bedroom upstairs.

There was a two-car garage and in it was a small white Corvair with red seats. Mom's new car. We were totally psyched. Mom, however, was shocked. Her reaction, though a bit cloaked with the thrill of all that was happening, was expected. *"But Peter, I don't know how to drive."* Dad smiled knowingly; *"Tess, I've hired a driving instructor to teach you."* After the tour of our new home and standing on the back patio overlooking a massive lush green yard, mom decided she could live off of Exit 27.

We moved. I was in the fifth grade and Perry, my older brother, was in the eighth grade. We were enrolled in St. Joseph's Catholic School, then taught by Franciscan Nuns. My first grade teacher from Utica, was transferred to St Josephs. It was reassuring to see a friendly face.

One day, sitting in my sixth-grade class, Sister Ceceilia asked that we open our Baltimore Catechism to page 33. The diagram on the page was extremely disturbing. There was a blue sky and clouds at the top of the page. An illustration of a church with the label *Catholic Church* was placed just below the sky with an arrow pointing to heaven sitting above the clouds. At the bottom of the page were flames. Another arrow pointing toward the flames were all other denominations. The caption at the top of the page read "The One True Church". I raised my hand to question the illustration. I asked, *"Does this mean anyone who isn't catholic is going to hell? That doesn't seem right."* Sister told me I was not to question our theology. I kept on, by asking, *"Why not?"* She then said my persistence was dangerously close to heresy. In those days, by the time you reached the sixth grade, you knew what a heretic was. I was asked to remain after class and my father was called down to the school. That was never good, but I couldn't let go of what I believed to be an unfounded and unfair assumption.

My father arrived dressed in his suit and tie, having left work, and not looking pleased. Sister Cecelia reported to him what had happened in class. He looked at me and asked why I was upset. I showed him the illustration and gave my point of view. Dad turned to Sister Cecelia and said, *"I hardly think my daughter's questions would label her a heretic. This illustration seems fairly provocative and would cause anyone*

4

pause." He was asked if he believed the Catholic church was the one true church. In my dad's inimitable style, he said, "*It's my true church and the one my wife and I are raising our family in. That said, I have taught all of my children to question. I think we need to have better answers to these questions and more tolerance.*" Sister Cecelia was not at all happy with my dad's response. She told him she would take it up with Sister Superior and have her get back to him.

When we left school that day. I asked Dad what he thought would happen; it was near the end of the year. My older brother was graduating from the 8th grade, his last year at St. Joseph's. Dad continued driving and looking ahead. "*You and your younger brother are going to public school next year.*" I looked at him and asked, "*What are we going to tell mom?*" He still didn't take his eyes off the road. "*We are not telling mom anything. I will discuss this with your mother.*" When we got home, mom asked what happened. Dad told her it was a misunderstanding, and he would discuss it with her later. I never learned how dad got mom to agree to public school, but that next year, all three of us were enrolled in the public school system. My younger brother in elementary, my older brother in high school, and I was in junior high.

The summer before we went to our new schools, my older brother became a caddy at the golf course across the street. He took to golf like a duck takes to water. By the end of the season, he was the most sought-after caddy, and a pretty good golfer. He scored a hole in one his second season!

Winters were pretty severe in upstate New York. Amsterdam was no exception. Both my brothers were excellent athletes, and avid skiers on the golf course hills —me, not so much.

I needed a winter pastime. I noticed moms and dads coming over to the course with thermoses filled with hot chocolate for their kids. It gave me an idea. At 12 years old, I had outgrown my little red wagon. My younger brother was no longer interested in it. I asked my dad if he could take off the wheels and make it into a sleigh. I told him my idea. Make hot chocolate at home with the instant packets mom discovered in the grocer. Fill the large, insulated coffee dispenser mom used for parties and set up a movable stand for the skiers. He was all in! We bought disposable hot cups with lids, boxes of hot chocolate packets from the church distributor, a large foam cord board and a ledger book. My dad filled in the ledger with my initial investment in red. We made a sign on the foam cord board with a wood tripod to set it on. I was in business and over the moon!

My weekends consisted of Saturdays from 10 – 3 and Sundays from 2 – 4. Many families went to church on Sunday morning and the custom in those days was to eat a Sunday dinner at noon.

At the close of business on my first Sunday I came home with $27.85. I was rich! Until dad pulled out the ledger with the itemized initial investment and the cost of replenishing my inventory. He handed me $8.22.

I immediately started to moan, at which point he explained the concept of *the cost of doing business*. The good news was, as he put it, I would make more the following weekend. My initial investment for retrofitting the wagon, buying the materials for the sign and the large insulated hot chocolate dispenser was a one-time only capital expense.

I worked for two years on the golf course happily making and saving money. I had accumulated quite a stash. My third winter, I arrived with my wagon sleigh in hand and noticed two adults in the golf course snack bar selling hot chocolate with marshmallows, and hot dogs with all the trimmings. Portable heaters were set up and there was a line of parents and kids waiting to place orders. My first reaction was pure shock. I was gob-smacked. Then I got really mad. Kids were still coming up to my wagon and buying from me, but my heart wasn't in it. These big people were stealing my customers! I went home early, threw myself on the rug in the front foyer and had a full-blown meltdown. My mom didn't know what to do. Dad was still at work and I was ballistic. Mom tried to console me to no avail. I finally went up to my room and shut myself in until Dad came home. My older brother told him what happened. He knocked on my door and I gave him a halfhearted, '*come in*''. He started out by saying it was a compliment to my entrepreneurship that the golf course felt the business I started was a worthwhile endeavor. He also said competition was inevitable and I needed to come up with a way to compete. I did have loyal customers. Many of them still came up to my wagon. I didn't have hotdogs. But we both knew that wasn't the only drawback. Later at supper, my younger brother offered to help. I was always a little jealous of his dexterity and well, I wasn't sure I wanted his help.

Dad had to remind me that my competition was the other guy, not my younger brother. In any case, Frank, who could ski perfectly without poles, had the notion of putting the money belt I used around his waist and skiing down the hill with two cups of hot chocolate in hand. Delivering hot drinks directly to skiers meant they didn't have to come up the hill to the snack bar or me. The golf course terrain was hilly and offered a combination of cross country and downhill. No ski lifts. Once you moved down, you could keep going across the course.

Having the hot drinks available for purchase on the spot was a big plus. It worked. Of course, I had to give my brother a small percentage of the profit, but it was the only way I could compete. I guess I was a nuisance because the big guys offered to buy me out and have me work for them. I conceded to being acquired and well, that was my winter job till I turned 15. The one thing they liked about me was my ability to form relationships and give each customer a special experience. I remembered names, and things they told me. I was great with the dads and moms who skied with their kids. By the way, that has stayed with me through the years. I genuinely care that people feel appreciated and listened to. We all matter.

At 15 I was able to secure working papers. My dad's store manager at Sears put me on the catalog desk at Christmas. My second season I was the number one booker. Mr. Pelitier, the store manager, asked me what I attributed my success to. I told him that mostly women came in at Christmas to shop for gifts from the catalog. They would buy their husbands shirts, ties, belts, and socks. During my first season, I noticed these purchasers kept coming back after Christmas with a '*Don't tell my wife that I brought these back.*' The second season, I got my wives to

buy Craftsman tools for the do-it-yourself guys or grown-up toys for the not so grown-up men. When a woman would say, 'But *my husband has so many tools,'* my answer was always the same. *"A man who loves to work with his hands, can never have too many tools."* Turns out I was right. Nothing came back!

New Beginnings and Coming of Age

When we moved to Wilbraham, MA in my senior year, I decided I needed a change of pace on the work front. I was also working hard to get into a good college. My mom often took me with her to the hair salon. She trusted my opinion. I was good with hair and makeup. She also took me shopping with her. I had a flair for fashion and knew what looked good on her and what didn't. This gave me the idea to do hair and makeup for women who didn't have time or couldn't afford to go to the salon. I would go to their homes, style their hair, and do their makeup for weekend dinners or events. I got really good at it and made pretty good weekend money. It beat babysitting, and it paid more.

After I graduated high school, I attended Boston University. It was wonderful to be in a big city. I loved it! I was meant to live an urbane lifestyle. I got a part time job at the new Lord & Taylor in the Prudential Center. In 1967, Lord & Taylor was a fashion-forward Manhattan-based department store. It was a big deal to bring L&T to Boston. All the dames of Boston shopped there. I saw Audrey Hepburn on the escalator, waited on Judy Garland and sold her a Rosanna sweater. The Sheraton was next door and purchased goods were beautifully wrapped, then hand carried over to the doormen who sent them with the bellmen to the rooms of the elite clientele visiting Boston.

Waiting on Judy Garland was a huge deal. My 15 minutes of fame, however, turned out to be memorable but not notable. In the 50's and 60's a woman took pride in being a size 12. I know, right? Believe it or not, size six was the smallest size in women's ready-to-wear and size five was the smallest size in what was then known as junior's ready-to-wear. Ms. Garland was very frail and thin. She came in with a "Dandy"[1] well-dressed younger man. She asked for a size 12 Rosanna sweater. I took her over to the sweaters and suggested she try on a size eight. She became quite agitated and told me she always wore a size 12 and didn't need to try it on. I took the size 12 out of the case, unfolded it and held it up to her. "Ms. Garland you'll swim in this". She asked to see my supervisor, whom she told in no uncertain terms, that I was impertinent. I was then asked by the manager of the department to wrap up the size 12 sweater and charge it to Ms. Garland's account. I did as I was told. When I put through the charge, I got a call from credit. I was asked to inform Ms. Garland that the sweater along with her other purchases would be sent over to her hotel. She left me to it. Minutes later I got a call from credit and was told to put the sweater back in stock. I asked why? "*Ms. Garland is over her credit limit,*" is what I was told. Later my manager told me she was essentially broke.

At the time of this writing, Rene Zelwinger was awarded an Oscar for her performance in *Judy*. Worth watching. I can tell you firsthand, her characterization and affect was spot on!

Two lessons learned; never argue with a customer, and not everything is how it appears. That experience stuck with me throughout my career.

After graduation, I was hired for the executive training program at the new Saks Fifth Avenue, Prudential Center in Boston. The store was exquisite and a significant step up from Lord & Taylor. After completing my initial training, I was assigned a post as manager of couture accessories and women's blouses. There I was surrounded by Judith Lieber belts and handbags, Bottega Veneta, Louis Vuitton and Chanel.

The blouse department ran the length of half of the second floor. There were sections of designer blouses from organza to satin, broadcloth shirts and cases of jabots. Jabots were an elaborate accessory of lace or satin falling in ruffles and attached or pinned to a neckband or collar.

Ms. Nan was the buyer for the designer belts and handbags and Ms. Janet was the buyer for women's blouses. Nan Edlestein was flamboyant,

---

[1] Bishop, John Peale, *"The Golden Age of The Dandy."* Vanity Fair Magazine, Sept 1920. *(https://archive.vanityfair.com/article/1920/09/01/the-golden-age-of-the-dandy)*

dressed in full skirts and gypsy blouses with bangle bracelets and dangling earrings. She was a force of nature. Beautiful, fun and totally unconventional. Ms. Nan taught me to go with my gut, take risks, and tap into my creative soul.

Ms. Janet looked like a schoolmarm. She wore dark gray shin length skirts and starched white shirts with dark jabots. She wore glasses with beaded eyeglass holder straps low on her nose.

I don't think I was ever told her last name or if I just don't remember it, but I remember her. Ms. Janet was stern, conservative, and painted by the numbers. She taught me the importance of using a step-by-step process. This was years before Lean Six Sigma. Ms. Janet understood attention to detail. She made a distinction I have never forgotten; "Attention to detail is not the same as being immersed in detail." The latter is about not knowing how to separate the wheat from the chaff. Her favorite line was, "Don't take shortcuts until you learn the long way home." Unlike Ms. Nan, Ms. Janet was not in favor of trusting your gut. She saw that as a secondary data point which should be filtered through data, experience, and know-how. Oddly enough, these two very different women were friends. They genuinely liked each other and had a mutual respect for one another. I think Ms. Nan was the only person who could make Ms. Janet laugh. It was always fun to watch.

After completing my second year at Saks, Ms. Nan recommended me for a promotion and asked if I was willing to relocate to Manhattan. I wasn't ready for such a big move. When I look back on that decision, I think I chickened out. I should have bitten the bullet and said yes!

At the beginning of my third year, I became friends with the cosmetics department manager. She ran a vast department and was totally energized by the constant change and glamor of it all. I remember a visit from industry moguls Charles Revson, the founder of Revlon, Estee Lauder, and Helena Rubinstein. I overheard Estee, who was dressed to the nines—complete with hat and gloves—asking Charles Revson if he had slept in his suite. They both laughed. He was eccentric and didn't seem to care. It was crazy.

I later asked my friend if she could put me in touch with one of these cosmetic companies. I wanted to work for one of them. She landed me an interview at Revlon. Unfortunately, because I had no direct cosmetic experience, the interviewer could not offer me a job. He also told me women generally worked behind the counter, or as makeup artists, not selling the product. When I asked why, his response was that since women wore cosmetics it biased them toward the products. At that time the sales force, sales managers, regional managers, and national sales managers were all men.

I later met with someone who had previously worked at Revlon. She was a makeup artist who had heard about an ex-Revlon executive leasing the franchise for Mary Quant cosmetics in the United States. Mary Quant invented the miniskirt and pantyhose. She had just licensed her name to Gala Cosmetics out of London and consulted with them on a line of cosmetics for young fashionable women—demographic age 17 – 35. I interviewed with Jack Winters, President of the U.S. Franchise.

Jack was amazing! We instantly hit it off. He offered me the New England Sales territory working for Kevin Francis and Sy Solkine. I met with both guys for final approval. They told me Jack had a vision for a different business model. He wanted to sell Quant as an accessory in Junior departments of department stores and to boutiques, which were becoming quite popular. What this meant was Jack was closing out our presence in cosmetic departments and major pharmacies. He said we had to establish a unique identity and not be "just another makeup line." Jack designed a free-standing black art deco unit. The unit was 4'7" tall and housed $1,200.00 worth of eye shadow, eyeliner, lipstick, blush, and mascara. The line was fashion forward. Colors were deep and dramatic and had crazy names, like Jeepers Peepers, and Liplicious…

My territory consisted of all of New England north to the Canadian border, and all of upstate New York west to Buffalo. In the 18 months I worked as the rep for New England, I closed out our line in 22 pharmacies, and opened 37 boutiques. In addition, opened three department stores headquartered in New England: Jordan Marsh and Filene's in Boston, and G Fox in Hartford, CT.

To get the line kick-started, I went back to my high school days of doing women's makeup and hair. I would schedule a demo day in the boutiques and department stores whenever I visited to replenish the inventory. The owners of the boutiques would put out a flier and let their customers know when I was coming. When I arrived, there would be a line of young women of all ethnic backgrounds waiting for their makeover. I started with Mary Quant mid-year 1973, and by 1975 I moved to Manhattan and became the national sales manager reporting directly to Jack Winters. Together with Kevin and Sy, we built a $10 million business. Today that would equate to a $50 million business. A solid performance for a startup!

Jack Winters picked up where my dad left off and taught me how to be a successful entrepreneur. These are the five rules of thumb he lived by:

1. In a negotiation when everything is said, the first one who talks loses.
2. There are two times you can afford to be strong, when you have nothing to lose and when you have everything to lose.
3. No business is always better than bad business.
4. Never hire ahead of revenue—don't spend money you don't have.
5. Give people who call you a few minutes of your time—you never know...

Rule number 5 was about people you meet along the way who may have found themselves out of work and needing a bit of advice. Someone you don't know who was referred by someone you do know, and, lastly, a stranger with a proposal for your business.

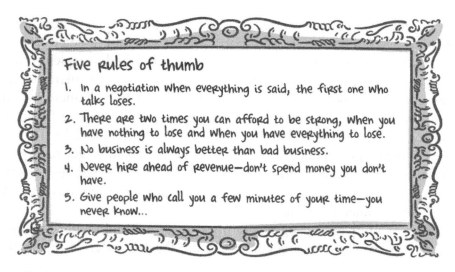

Five rules of thumb

1. In a negotiation when everything is said, the first one who talks loses.
2. There are two times you can afford to be strong, when you have nothing to lose and when you have everything to lose.
3. No business is always better than bad business.
4. Never hire ahead of revenue—don't spend money you don't have.
5. Give people who call you a few minutes of your time—you never know...

Jack's view was when you treat people the way you would want to be treated, the universe will be on your side. His version of the Golden Rule—and he lived it.

I remember being in a taxi on our way to the airport. A woman with a flat tire standing by her car on the East River Drive looked very stressed. Jack stopped our cab, got out and changed her tire. The meter was running and the cabby was pretty taken aback. Here was Jack, dressed in a suit and tie changing this woman's tire. She hugged Jack and was so grateful. The look of relief on this woman's face was so moving. Jack hopped back in the cab and thanked the driver for waiting. The driver looked in his rearview mirror and said rather sheepishly, *"well the meter was running"*. About 10 minutes from the airport, the cabby turned the meter off. Jack smiled and thanked him. Later he said, *"when it's in your power to help someone don't wait for the next guy, just do it."* That was years before the phrase, *pay it forward*[2] came into play.

Shortly after I moved to Manhattan, I met my future husband. Only a year later, the Gala Cosmetics Group came to N.Y. to meet with Jack. The next thing I knew, Jack packed up his office and the London guys took over.

---

[2] Hyde, Catherine Ryan. *Pay It Forward.* Simon & Schuster; Reissue edition. 23 Dec 2014

By that time, I had a full team of people working in sales and Jack had a full staff. The London guys basically told us Jack's licensing contract was up and they decided not to renew it. We asked why? We were dumbstruck by their answer; the company's revenue had exceeded their expectations. They had been looking for a way to break into the American market and Quant gave them the opportunity. Nothing against Jack, this was just business.

What the London guys underestimated was our bond with Jack and each other. Later that day, I reached Jack at home. He asked that we stay cool for a few weeks and he would be in touch. Three weeks later, Jack called. He had obtained the license for Biba Cosmetics out of London and was an investor. We were back in business. That night we met at Jack's apartment and worked out the details of what would become our new company. Jack's wife Lola worked on getting us new space and his former assistant was looking into phones, fax, and copy machines. One week later Jack's assistant, who now worked for the new guys, received a memo that they would be traveling to London the following week—leaving on Monday night and returning Thursday night. She booked their flights, alerted Jack and the rest of us of their plans. The following Tuesday after they left, the entire New York based team gave individual resignation letters to Rochelle, Jack's assistant. She facilitated the whole process, including having the staff outside of New York to fax their resignations to her. On Thursday while they were enroute to the airport, Rochelle sent our resignation letters to the Chairman of Gala Cosmetics in London. When the executives from London returned to their offices on Friday, everyone was gone. There were empty offices with rows of desks in the sales bullpen, all empty—the reception area was clean and empty also. We had beautiful offices on Fifth Avenue in the Six's building.

I can't imagine what the reaction was like when these guys came into the office and learned that their little coup backfired. Mary Quant in the U.S. went out of business a year later.

Biba did very well in its first six months. Many of our previous department store and boutique clients bought from us. It was Jack's vision they were buying into—selling cosmetics to a young demographic as an accessory to clothes, shoes, and handbags. Unfortunately, we were reliant on inventory from London and our investors. The recession hit, and we lost our funding. It was a very sad time. Jack had to close the U.S. operation. Most of the team went on to other cosmetic companies—we were highly sought after.

And Then There Were Two

I was at a crossroads. My soon-to-be-husband was extremely supportive but wanted me to find a position with less travel, since I had been traveling two to three weeks a month; he traveled, too, and we weren't always able to sync our travels.

A friend of a friend introduced me to a corporate officer at Xerox Corporation. Xerox was looking to hire four women to be on a management fast track. I couldn't imagine leaving the fashion and cosmetic business to join the copier company. The officer I met with asked that I meet with the Manhattan-based management staff to get a flavor for what I'd be signing up for, should I decide to join the company. Xerox stock was a thousand dollars a share at the time. There were four major districts in Manhattan. The opportunity offered a great starting salary, considerably more than I was making, minimal travel, and sales, finance and management training commensurate with an MBA. Not to mention, the four women would be the first females to be managers in a tech company largely populated by men.

After several rounds of interviews, I decided to take the offer seriously.

Ron and I were married on October 8, 1977, at the New Canaan Inn. The corporate officer who initially spoke with me lived in New Canaan, CT. He came over the morning of my wedding scheduled to start at 1:00 PM, to offer me the job. There we were sitting on the terrace outside my room, me in electric rollers and a terry cloth robe having coffee. He offered me the job and I accepted.

From entrepreneur to corporate

I spent 23 years at Xerox. I worked with and for some amazing people. I often thought of Miss Janet. At Xerox, I learned the long way home. I became a savvy businessperson with the discipline and rigor you get from working in a large corporation. My entrepreneurial background gave me the courage to take risks and the ability to be a self-starter. I rose through the ranks quickly, but it was not without its challenges. There were many times when I asked myself, *what am I doing in this business*? I missed the excitement of a fashion environment and the creative aspects of working in an innovative business.

My first assignment at Xerox was leading a team in the Midtown West branch. The branch manager was not happy that I was assigned to his district. Of the four women, I was the only one hired from the outside and he resented that. The other three women, two of which were in sales in Midtown West, were also not happy I was put in the role. One was assigned to Midtown East, the other two to Uptown and Long Island.

My district manager realigned my sales team, giving the best assignments to a male peer he had promoted to the role. He left me with a challenging set of sales territories and reps. My first operations review took place 45 days after I started. One of my assignments was retail, which I was very familiar with, given my early career. Sears was in the process of closing their New York anchor store. They canceled all their N.Y. contracts and relocated their Xerox equipment to Chicago. I requested budget relief and was denied.

I asked one of my other peers if there was a relocation policy. One of the other sales managers was Black, and he took pity on me. He told me I should have received a relocation credit and suggested I call the national account manager to facilitate the credit. I did and the district manager got word of it and went ballistic! He called me into his office and handed me a written warning for insubordination. I asked him why on earth he was so angry. The revenue loss affected his bottom line as much as mine. If the equipment was simply being relocated, we shouldn't take the cancellation hit on our side. He basically dismissed me by saying I should have gone through him and proper channels. I was not getting a formal warning for the result; the ends simply didn't justify the means. He was out for me and I knew it. If the peer he had given the juicy territories to had done the same thing, he would have been rewarded.

The Ops review day came, I was 29% of my plan and extremely nervous.

When it was my turn, I put up my transparencies (slides) and got ripped to shreds by the region execs in the room. My district manager sat and watched. He said nothing in my defense. One of the execs, nicknamed *The Iceman,* asked me what kind of talent did it take to be 29% of plan? Everyone snickered, including Sans my newfound Black friend. At that point, I remembered one of Jack's five guiding rules from my days as national sales manager for Mary Quant. *There are two times you can afford to be strong; when you have everything to lose and nothing to lose.* I was in both those positions. I lifted my head, threw my shoulders back and in my lowest voice, calmly answered rhetorically. *"If after 45 days in territory I was 29% of my plan, would you attribute that to my expertise?"* There was silence in the room. You could hear a pin drop. One of the other region execs, David Bliss, broke the silence. *"She has a point, gentlemen,"* he said. *"Do you have a plan for how you will recoup your losses and grow future revenue?"* I was off to the races. I presented my plan in detail—to include the relocation credit the national account manager was working on. I ended the year on plan. I didn't break any records, but it took a herculean effort to get there. The Northeast Region President recognized me at the regional sales meeting.

> There are two times you can afford to be strong; when you have everything to lose and nothing to lose.

After my first Ops review, I called the other three women and gave them a heads up on the questions that were asked, and the overall tenor of the players in the room. It wasn't long after that we became friends, and I was accepted as an "insider". I felt it was really important not to allow us to be pitted against each other. We had too much to lose.

Stepping into Startups

As I progressed in my career, I was given opportunities to run new businesses—startups inside the corporation. Through doing so, I became a strong leader and was well respected by my peers, bosses, and direct reports.

In 1993 I was asked to join the corporate executive team. There was a big movement on empowerment. A word that was just coming into vogue—it didn't even exist in the dictionary then. The CEO's Chief of Staff heard me speak at an internal conference. He liked what I had to say and asked Anne Mulcahy, then CHRO, to bring me on board. I was appointed to the role of Chief Transformation Officer. While empowerment was just coming into vogue, transformation was like speaking a foreign language.

The Executive Leadership Team was working on forward plans for what was coined *Year 2000*. This initiative crossed technology, corporate infrastructure, products, solution selling and customer service. Enterprise Resource Planning, affectionately referred to as ERP, was rampant across major corporations. Xerox decided to re-engineer its four core processes. Michael Hammer was the process reengineering guru of the time. Xerox was all in. Our biggest challenge at the time was tackling all four processes at once. A decision we would look back on and seriously regret. Everything was in play.

Anne Mulcahy was asked to spearhead this initiative with our newly appointed Chief Information Officer. Each process had a process owner, all of whom were senior executives, EVPs with oversight for enterprise-wide organizations—each of them were men. The CIO and CHRO were in advisory roles, both were women.

The four core processes were identified as:

1. Time to market
2. Market to collection
3. Integrated supply chain
4. Post-sale service

The process integration meetings going on among the four process owners were highly charged. Each owner needed to outline in detail the handoff steps from time to market to post-sale service. If there was a lag in getting a product ready for market, folks taking our product to customers would suffer a lag time which would hurt revenue projections from new product launches. The debates among the group became legendary. It was every man for himself!

Anne came back from one of these meetings looking like she had the weight of the world on her shoulders. She came into my office and asked me to start facilitating these meetings as part of my remit. Her logic, which I couldn't fault, was that reengineering these processes would ultimately fall under *transformation.* And so, it began.

When I entered the room at the next meeting, Anne introduced me as the newly appointed Chief Transformation Officer. That got some serious looks. The Chief Engineer flippantly said, *"What on earth does that mean?"* Anne took a breath and was about to respond. I beat her to it, and simply said, *"I guess it means that if you don't change, you're under arrest."* That got a laugh. Anne sighed with relief and left me to it. When Anne left, several of the men at the table asked what my role would be in their sessions. My response bought me some time; "I've spent my entire career in client facing roles. I know our customers, what they expect and what we need to do to scale and grow our business. Think of me as a filter for the reengineering efforts you are all working on. I am the voice of the customer."

In subsequent sessions, I brought video clips of customer interviews. These were very well received and taken seriously. Customers felt we were difficult to do business with. Too many complex procedures. We were so focused on our internal functions and structures that we were doing business with ourselves. I often referred to it as *playing office*. The CIO took a major liking to me and began incorporating my guidance into the work of the group. She is, to this day, a dear friend. We did good work together. The Chief Engineer was exceptionally smart, very accomplished, and intimidating to the group. Every time he dismissed the ideas of others, the room would go radio silent.

At one of these sessions, I called a time-out and inserted a 15-minute break.

I quietly leaned over to our Chief Engineer and asked if I could have a minute. He led me out of the conference room and asked if he was the reason we took the break. I thanked him for his awareness and said actually yes. "You have an amazing intellect. It is a God given gift. You can use it to enlighten others or as a weapon. Your choice." He came back from break and was quiet the remainder of the session. We became buds and that led to mutual respect. The team started working together with an appreciation for diverse points of view. I fell into a facilitation rhythm that later became a core capability and skill set.

Six months into the role, I proposed to Anne the formation of a new function; *The Center for Business Transformation*. I took open space below the executive floor and had our real-estate people open the walls with glass partitions that looked out on a tree-filled indoor courtyard. The intention was an open concept that gave visibility to us and our work. People dropped in to collaborate on different projects.

Anne introduced me to Shirley Edwards, (who at the time was running Corporate Audit), and some people from PARC, (Palo Alto Research Center). We agreed to partner in the Center and formed a loose alliance. Shirley and her assistant moved into the open space. The folks from PARC worked with us when they visited HQ. and they made space for us at PARC. We were able to bring future-oriented research from PARC'S Practice Labs to guide our year 2000 transformation strategy. It was extremely gratifying. Much of what we see today in collaborative technologies and practices were conceived at PARC long ago.

The Center was a pivotal force for change. At the beginning of 2000, I accepted an offer to establish a Center for Business Transformation at

Gartner. That's where I met Gavin. A year later we founded *fassforward* Consulting Group, *The How Company*.

Our Consulting firm was born out of the work started at Xerox and later brought to Gartner.

As of July 2023, we have been in business for 22 years. Our team has expanded to roughly 20 talented people from diverse backgrounds, disciplines, and subject matter expertise. Due to the global pandemic we have successfully changed our business model from live face-to-face client engagements to live online and virtual engagements.

For me, my journey has always been about change. From the move as a child to exit 27 on the NYS thruway to the move to Massachusetts in my senior year in high school and all the moves thereafter.

I've met amazing women and men along the way and continue to learn from a variety of people from all walks of life.

Chapter Two

It All Started With Chocolate

It all started with chocolate which became my first book, *The Chocolate Conversation*. Many of you picked up the book because you found the title intriguing. You're probably asking the question, "What is a leadership conversation? How can a leadership conversation unpack *chocolate conversations*? Why is that important? So far, so good. Now you've started a conversation with me—one I really want to have with you. What if I told you everything regarding your leadership, the market leadership of your company, followership, and change happens in the conversation? What if I went so far as to say the single factor that determines success or failure is the conversation? Still listening? Okay. For those of you who read the first book, it's been awhile. And for those of you who didn't, here's a quick summary on how this all got started.

Bring your own Chocolate

A few years after I graduated from college, I was invited to a "Death by Chocolate" party. It was a BYOC invitation, Bring your own Chocolate to share with everyone. What a hoot! I prepared my award-winning, killer chocolate cake, figuring I'd be the hit of the party—and off I went. I expected the usual suspects: chewy double-fudge brownies, chocolate chunk cookies, and chocolate mousse. I'd set my sights too low—when I arrived, there before me was a seven-foot table laden with every conceivable chocolate confection I could imagine: Éclairs nestled among soufflés, truffles, hand-dipped fruit—a veritable chocolate lover's paradise. Alas! The only thing missing was the magic potion to make all the calories disappear before the afterglow of the evening appeared on my derriere.

Competition was stiff and the conversations about chocolate were intense: texture, density, aroma, percentage of cacao; these were serious chocolate snobs! One very slim woman declared, "When I indulge, it's got to be high quality—something I can savor long after I've eaten it." The guy standing next to me rolled his eyes, and under his breath said, "When I want chocolate, a Snickers bar will do just fine." She shot him an indignant look and stalked off.

What we all had in common was our love of chocolate—and that's where it ended. Once we got below the surface, everyone had their own ideas about what chocolate meant to them—and no one was budging from *their* standard, no matter what.

Several years later, I was in an all-company meeting listening to our CEO lay out the annual new direction for the business. After the meeting, we all brought the plan back to our respective teams. As the plan worked its way through team meetings, town halls, company newsletters, and water-cooler talk, the original message got lost. We could all agree while flying at 30,000 feet and looking down at the broad landscape, but everyone had their own perceptions on the ground when we became preoccupied with the look of our own neighborhoods, so to speak. As multiple interpretations of the plan were set in motion, we were left with a lot of unintended outcomes—and disappointing results. The CEO was frustrated, and other leaders were left scratching their heads.

Suddenly, I thought of the "Death by Chocolate" party. We had all gone to that party with a common objective—bring chocolate, eat chocolate, and be happy—only to be separated by our different interpretations or standards for what constituted "ideal" chocolate. What happened at that party was happening in our company—everyone had a different interpretation for what they thought the plan meant and how they would bring it to their teams to implement. One person's soufflé was another's Snickers bar. I realized if a simple concept like chocolate could generate so many different opinions, attitudes, and points of view, how many more would occur when a complex strategy was at stake? When images and points of view differ and we can't communicate a consistent message, we wind up with a "meltdown": The outcome ends up looking like Snickers, truffles and souffle all mixed together; in other words, something one would buy at a drugstore, a premium chocolatier, or order at the beginning of a meal in a gourmet restaurant. What we have is completely different types and standards of chocolate—the result isn't what was expected, and everyone is confused and disappointed.

I see this problem all the time, and I'm sure you do, too. People get a thought in their minds after they hear something and they picture what it means to them. They talk with others based on their own understanding and they agree to take actions based on that understanding—without considering how the originator of the message intended it to come across. To them, there was no original message—there is only the message in their point of view—what they *thought* they heard. As a result, the original intention breaks down and—like the woman who walked away at the chocolate party—employees walk away confused and frustrated over these misunderstandings.

Have you ever wondered why two-thirds of all mergers fail to produce the value of the two stand-alone companies—let alone the additional benefits promised? Companies lose billions of dollars over *chocolate conversations*. Everyone talks at the "chocolate" level—what I'm going to call the "Worldview" here, and they agree they have something in common—the objective or result. Then, the individual points-of-view kick in (what we'll call the Standards) about what to do and how to do it—and that's different from team to team and person to person. Everything melts down into a morass of upsets and complaints, the unmet needs I'll be calling Concerns in this book.

"Life Happens when you're making other plans"[1] — *John Lennon*

I knew I had something to offer when my former boss, Ann Mulcahy, who at the time was Chief of Staff and later became the CEO of Xerox, told me other than my day job of running a business, I had a unique talent. I could "bring a diverse group of people together and get them on the same page." I wasn't brought into Xerox to do that, but, when the company decided to make a significant change to our business model, Anne asked me to do just that and appointed me the "Chief Transformation Officer." That was nearly thirty years ago. As I said before, the word "transformation" was not in the corporate lexicon as it is today. People had no idea what a Chief Transformation Officer was, much less what I was meant to do. At the time, I'm not sure I knew. So, when asked, I simply smiled and said, "I guess if you don't change, you're under arrest." That provided enough levity to give me time to figure out what it was I *could* do to shape and facilitate the transformation of the "Copier Company" to the Document Solutions Company we wanted to become. That gig lasted five years and was the genesis for my company, *fassforward* Consulting Group, a business transformation boutique that Gavin McMahon and I founded twenty-two years ago.

What matters to me is that people "get gotten." Every human being wants to be understood and validated. I've known this from my earliest years—when, as the "middle" child, I learned how to stand in the middle and not only survive but understand everyone around me—and get them to understand each other. I'm fascinated by people and their interactions. I love listening to conversations, even when they're happening at a table next to me in a restaurant. My husband often asks me if I want to join the other table. That's when we both laugh, and I share the insights I've picked up from eavesdropping.

I hear not only what is said, but the silent conversation going on in someone's head—what they meant to say or wanted to say and couldn't. I often act as a proxy and say out loud what I think I've heard. It frees people to speak their minds in a way that respects another's point of view. I reframe conversations and situations so everyone can understand everyone else, and I often move people to make a difference for themselves and each other. Growing up, I was told by someone very dear to me that I was a "translator." I didn't know I was developing a system for myself, but it's worked over and over again in every area of my life ever since.

That's why Chocolate Conversations resonate so much for me—I get that people come from different walks of life, experiences, and places, and where they come from defines them on a profound level. It's not simply what they believe, it is who they think they are. For a leader to make a difference all the way through the levels of their organizations, they must listen to, and understand where people at each of those levels are coming from and communicate with them in a language they understand, so they can build real consensus. Leaders have to be more than "good communicators", they need to be *translators*.

Taking it to the Next Level

I've lived through several company-wide transformation efforts as a senior executive. In my consulting practice, I've helped many clients figure out how to take their business to the next level. You can't get there by doing more of what you did yesterday. You must constantly reinvent yourself, and that means "change." Once I had the realization that all-company meetings at Xerox were a *chocolate conversation*, I began to see *chocolate conversations* causing misunderstandings and serious meltdowns every time companies had to do something other than business as usual.

Let's face it, we *are* going to see ever-increasing waves of change in our digital, global economy. Change is really the only constant we face. Business as usual is a certain recipe for failure—*You're either growing or you're dying*—that's never been more true than it is today.

I guarantee that—*right now*—your competitors are thinking about the same three questions global leaders of well-known brands, not-for-profit organizations, and—yes, even nations are asking:

How do we grow? Can we scale?
Can we do it productively?

The question they often forget to ask and the one the success of the other three depends on is—*Are we relevant?*

The answer is always "something's gotta' change,", and if something has to change, then someone has to lead people through the change. People have to understand what is being asked of them, and they have to see themselves in the picture.

This is why knowing what *chocolate conversations* are, how to recognize them, and how to clarify them is so important. You simply cannot change and grow your company while you're having *chocolate conversations*. Radical change absolutely guarantees countless *chocolate conversations* at every level of your company every day. This was further exacerbated by the pandemic resulting in people working remotely.

There *is* a way to have conversations that resonate for every person at every level, where each one sees themselves as an important player in the new game. AND there is a way to put change in context, get through it—and do it well. Here's how…

There are four significant conversations in this book

The first conversation is the one you have had with yourself throughout your professional journey. I share my conversation to get you thinking about yours.

The second conversation is about ***change in companies***. We will look at what works and what doesn't. Why, you can't just use the wrapper of some other company's playbook, business model and organization design. When I say it that way, people nod their heads; but it's surprising how many companies do this. Most importantly, you can't stand still. Even if you are successful today, *the path from industry leadership to receivership is brutally short.* You have to find what matters inside and outside your company and translate that into the recipe for your relevance and growth five years down the road.

The third conversation is about ***leading change***. Change starts with you. You're the one who has to make things happen. You have to be relevant to your team, your company, your company's strategy, and your customers. You have to figure out how you grow and scale within your company as you help your company grow and scale. *You are the translator, moving from chocolate conversations to leadership conversations* that start with a deep understanding of where everyone is and how everyone fits in order to get the company where it needs to be. Lastly conversation four is about **making change happen**. It gives you some practical things to do so you can change your company and achieve the relevance, growth, and scale you need to be a market leader. In a sense, making things happen as a leader is straightforward. Change happens in the conversation, and there are only two conversations that matter—conversations that *reframe your people's thinking* and conversations that *move people to action.* Every other conversation is noise in the system. and the roar of that noise can be deafening.

The point of my first book is to know when you are having a *chocolate conversation* and what to do about it. *The point of this book is how to have a Leadership Conversation,* how to reframe the conversation, and how to get people to act.

Chapter Three

Leadership Happens in the Conversation—Or Not

A great example of failed leadership came from a senior executive client who struggled with motivating his team. We first met in his stylish, chrome and glass office. I looked around and noted leadership books filled the shelves. Clearly, he was looking for the "secret sauce" that would make him a great leader. He had a brilliant mind—that was apparent from our first telephone conversation. In the same discussion, he claimed his team couldn't keep up with him. He was frustrated, and I guessed his team was frustrated as well.

He took me through the challenges his group faced and proved to be very smart and also very expressive about his goals. I asked questions to help him to further articulate his vision, but something didn't sit right with me.

Listening to the points in his vision is what I do for a living, so I could read between the lines and grasp the whole picture. However, the very fact that I had to "read between the lines" at all meant he wasn't speaking as simply as he could to communicate his vision for his company or what he wanted from his staff. His conversation was peppered with what I call *corporate-speak:* he wanted his people to be "information facilitators" and "system advisors" rather than sales representatives. I noted that he spoke over the ends of my sentences as if he couldn't wait for me to finish before he continued what *he* wanted to say—always a sign for me that someone is not really listening.

We met several times before he agreed to let me see him in action. I attended a staff meeting and watched and listened as he spoke to his team. I noticed he was already trying to apply some of what we'd talked about. He made a huge effort to incorporate my direction about speaking simply; however, the more he talked, the more he regressed into his normal corporate-babble. He waved away the few brave hands that went up at the beginning of his speech—soon, everyone gave up and there were no more raised hands.

He spoke for one hour during which he touched on a number of "key priorities." His message was convoluted and unclear. I watched his people as he spoke—many rubbed their eyes and foreheads, some looked at each other wide-eyed, and I detected slight shrugs between people which signaled defeat.

At the very end, he asked for feedback. The silence was deafening. They had long since given up trying to understand what he wanted of them. Some of them in the back actually put their heads in their hands. When he concluded the meeting, no one seemed to know the meeting was over. They left, after the hour-long meeting, not knowing or understanding what was expected of them—that was clear from the bowed heads, slumped shoulders, and quiet air of resignation as they logged off.

When he and I reconvened, I shared my observations. He bristled a bit. I could see he prided himself on being an articulate, intelligent executive. No argument there—he was certainly intelligent. Among his peers, he probably was articulate. What he wasn't, however, was a good communicator.

Good communicators, and therefore good leaders, translate complexity into simple straightforward language that moves people. When people are moved, they are motivated to act. Therein lies the "secret sauce" he was looking for in all of those books on his bookshelves.

Leadership Happens in the Conversation—Or Not

Leaders drive results through people. For many years, I've been telling my teams, my colleagues, and my clients that leadership happens—or doesn't happen—in the conversation. As a leader, you have a practical job to do. People need to pull together to meet targets and perform on behalf of the company and their customers. Shareholders and stakeholders want to be kept informed on trends and projections. It's all about people, the ones who work for you, the ones you work for, and the ones who buy from you.

Within the conversation is where you have the greatest daily impact as a leader. What we say—and what people hear—can be very different. What we hear and think we understand can be misinterpreted.

I have seen significant levels of controversy in companies attempting to adopt a new technology that cannibalizes the core business, a shift that always causes different points of view to emerge. Changes in compensation benefit plans, and other reward systems, are also fodder for controversy since they affect people on a personal level. Organizational changes can result in people losing power and influence—again, a positive change for the company that may leave some people with ego wounds to lick. I don't have to tell you how brutal those conversations can be.

Leaders have to have those conversations—sometimes one on one, in small groups or in a public forum. Conversations can be informal or in public forums in front of large audiences. Some conversations are televised like webinars that CEOs have, with far flung global teams or even State of the Union Addresses.

There's no room for confusion—everyone has to come out of the conversation knowing three things:

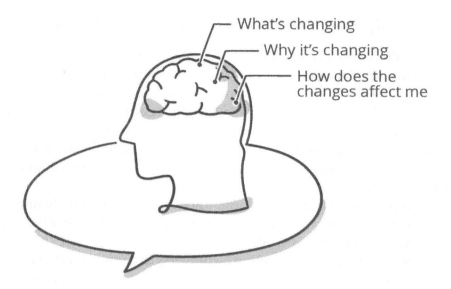

- What's changing
- Why it's changing
- How does the changes affect me

Having an indirect or what I refer to as the "non conversation" lacks leadership direction and clarity. This erodes people's confidence, performance, and faith in the company, or organization. Therefore, making the most brilliant "change initiatives" die long, painful, expensive deaths. Ultimately, everyone suffers, and the company struggles to regain its footing.

At the writing of this book, we were in the midst of a Coronavirus pandemic, requiring most people to work remotely and most conversations to happen virtually. That added a whole other layer to understanding and interpretation. Leaders needed to be more aware of simple, straightforward language that offered warmth and motivation because we wanted to move people to action. Now that we're returning to offices, all of that is just as important now. There are two conversations that exist in leadership. Conversations which help people to understand what's going on and conversations which move them to action.

Having conversations that truly communicate intentions are vital to achieving your goals, and to surfacing the potential concerns of others. It is so much the lifeblood of an organization that it can be said, "Communication is to leadership what water is to life."

At the worldview level, almost everyone agrees communication is critical. When you go beyond paying lip service to this concept, and you begin to set standards for how you communicate, and with whom and with what frequency you can do more to effectively lead and move your company forward than with any other initiative.

Leadership happens in the conversation, and that conversation happens in the moment. When you manage a project or a process you often have time to plan. When you are suddenly confronted with an unknown, you have to act in the moment and respond. Those moments can define our leadership. Remember, too, that even when we are silent, we are communicating. People will read into your silence as well as your words.

I will go further and say communication is so central to leadership that once an individual becomes a leader, they no longer have the luxury of casual conversations. People hear everything. The casual conversation you have in the hall, or the off-the-cuff remark you make, could have significant ramifications.

As an example, when President Trump indicated that of course we are having more positive COVID-19 test results[3] because we are testing more. He casually said, "Maybe we should stop testing." While he said he meant it as a casual remark, it took on a life of its own.

In another example, I was talking to a client who was a Chief People Officer for an education company who wanted to convey the concern the company had for social justice. He spoke openly and very vulnerably about being a gay man.

He shared what it was like when gay marriage became acceptable in his particular state. Lastly, he spoke about how much flack they took as he struggled at the time to express to family members and friends

---

[3] Begley, Sharon. *"Trump said more Covid-19 testing 'creates more cases.' We did the math"*. STAT NEWS, 20 Jul 2020 *(https://www.statnews.com/2020/07/20/trump-said-more-covid19-testing-creates-more-cases-we-did-the-math/)*

that they had gone ahead and married. His message to the employees was an attempt to make himself vulnerable and relatable to the African American employees. However, it was taken poorly and referred to as a micro-aggression. Employees responded with essentially, "This isn't about you, it's about us." What he came to understand is you can never make a situation about you because it's translated as, "You're not hearing me."

These are both examples of how even the smallest comment, like the one by the former President can communicate volumes and how a well-intended speech can be taken as, "You're not listening."

Communication needs to be authentic. It's not about saying the right thing or using the right buzzwords. One might say all the right things, in the right tone of voice, and in the most positive manner, it doesn't mean their words will land as meaningful and true. Most people see right through someone who is talking in corporate speak or jargon. Speak straight, speak what you intend, speak from what you know to be true and people will respond with their own conviction, and you can then have a dialogue which is purposeful and moves people forward. For example, the gay leader could have made his personal story short and real, and then opened the conversation to what his African American employees experience and how they felt. This is more of what it means to be inclusive. Inclusion is a corporate initiative and now a function. It alone will never give people a sense of being included. Actions and our daily *leadership conversations* have the greatest impact.

If you think of every communication as a conversation, and you are authentic and open, people will respond to you. Even when they don't agree, they will feel they can express themselves, and then you'll know why they disagree. This is a good thing. If you know people disagree and you know *why*, you've opened a dialogue and can now resolve differences and align your people to you—then move forward.

You may not be the best presenter in the world, but if you are able to communicate in an open and conversational style, it creates receptivity—and people will respond. You know when people are responding when they give you feedback. This is how you uncover unmet needs. When you uncover and acknowledge peoples' unmet needs, obstacles fall away and you are left with a clear understanding which moves people into action.

Even the best communicators can be misinterpreted. It's important to communicate with the understanding that someone is on the receiving end of what you are saying. People are going to interpret what you have to say. Knowing this will cause you to stay focused and speak straight from the heart.

I've met my share of superstar leaders, and even they don't start out fully formed. Putting experience aside for the moment, the fundamental attributes that great leaders have is *the ability to convey a message to their followers to take action.*

Let's look at this for a moment. Napoleon, a short man with a grand vision, was able to conquer half of Europe. Winston Churchill, who successfully led England to resist Hitler during World War II, became a political outcast who spoke like he had a handful of marbles in his mouth. Golda Meir was a teacher from Wisconsin who helped establish a nation state and led Israel into the 21st century. Nelson Mandela and Dr. Martin Luther King both challenged discrimination in their societies despite being the targets of prejudice themselves. Rosa Parks sat on a bus, *in silence*, leading a change that significantly advanced the civil rights movement. Mother Teresa, through compassion and a tireless effort, communicated with her devotion and faith to make a difference for the victims of poverty in India.

All these leaders had courage, commitment, and vision. But, what really set them apart—what made them *leaders*—was their ability to convey a message to their followers that inspired action. They spoke from their hearts about what they believed. People responded and made those causes their own. What made these leaders effective was their ability to convey what was important to them and make it important to others.

Speaking naturally and authentically about what you believe in, whether it is a political position, a personal choice, or a business decision, will get the attention of your audience.

Chapter Four

M&A's: A Petri Dish for Chocolate Conversations

Hanging onto a business model that is no longer relevant and can't scale beyond where it is today is a recipe for slow growth and perpetual cost cutting. These old and out of date models are ripe for *chocolate conversations*. Customers are the first to let you know your company is standing still. This shows up in declining organic growth, customer retention losses, and missing new business targets.

When it comes to a corporate environment, employees want to work for successful, thriving companies, and customers want to do business with successful, thriving companies.

So, how do you do this?

Many companies do this with mergers and acquisitions. It is a fast way to add what you need. The rationale goes like this: "we have products and a distribution system that company X wants, and company Y has a technology and a delivery system that we need to grow. Let's get our companies together and we will dominate the market." This is a *1 + 1 = 3* deal—the whole is greater than the sum of its parts. The capabilities each company has are critical to both companies' long-term growth *beyond* what either of the companies could have achieved on their own.

The reality is, for two out of every three mergers, rather than 1 + 1 = 3, the story usually ends with 1 + 1 = minus 1. The merged companies perform way below expectations. On a people level, synergies fail to develop, key people leave, customers complain about dislocations in delivery, and value is lost. On a company level, scale fails to materialize, productivity falters, and companies shrink instead of growing.

Sometimes, companies lose their identity in mergers and their relevance evaporates right along with it. *Why?* It falls right back to the *Chocolate Conversation.* The respective companies come together because they bought into a common worldview. Once the deal is closed and the euphoria of the newly formed entity is behind everyone, they find their culture and standards are different, and they don't know how to get value from the new company.

The following chart outlines why two companies came together when they merged, and where the two companies often disconnected after the merger:

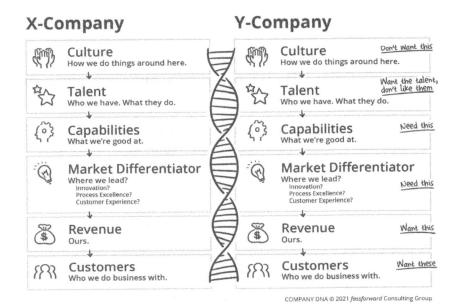

COMPANY DNA © 2021 *fassforward* Consulting Group

Both companies want the capabilities of the other to enhance their own, wanting to retain what is best about both of them, *and* to add new capacities to create that synergistic "greater whole." Both companies want to retain their own customers *and* both companies want to add new ones so the new company grows beyond what either of them could have done alone. These two pieces are where everyone agrees.

BUT—and this is a big but, their cultures are different, and culture begets language and the "how we do things around here." They basically didn't understand each other from the get-go. AND—that "different culture" hired talent which blended with their own culture and standard, not the others'. Each discovers they don't even like or appreciate the talent the other company brings to the table. Yet, it is this very talent who created the value for each of the companies in the first place.

In the two examples highlighted in this chapter, I'll discuss what happens when different cultures with conflicting standards come up against each other, and how to mitigate through that phase. We'll show you how to discover *what* you need to change and *how* you can drive change across your entire company, even if your company spans the globe.

Successful Mergers Turn Chocolate Conversations into Leadership Conversations

Estée Lauder Companies was fassforward's first account. I met and worked with Harvey Gideon when he was the head of R&D at Revlon and reconnected with him when he took over R&D at Estée Lauder. He brought me in and laid out their dilemma.

The strategy for the company was to acquire popular brands which attracted a broader, younger consumer so they could fill the void left open by their own customers' growing up. One of those brands was a hot, new, Canadian line, MAC cosmetics. MAC, or "Makeup Artist Cosmetics," had been founded in Toronto in 1984 to supply professional make-up artists. As a pleasant and profitable surprise, the company found a consumer base—and opened their first store in New York in 1991.

Estée Lauder Companies acquired MAC only seven years after that. It seemed the perfect product line to appeal to a younger demographic— MAC was famous for its dramatic color line and popularity among pop culture. It was miles away from the traditional upscale department store brands, the greatest of which was Este Lauder.

My first meeting was with Harvey, head of Research & Development for Estée Lauder, and his Chief Scientist, Shahan Nazar. Shahan talked to me about the challenges he faced bringing MAC's "first to market" young culture to Lauder's world-renowned, scientifically based, long-standing way of doing things. Shahan wanted to bring the best of both companies together. MAC would bring speed and new innovation to Lauder, and Lauder would bring scale and global presence to MAC.

One thing immediately caught my attention. I was having these conversations with Harvey and Shahan back in 2001, and the MAC acquisition had been completed in 1998. We were discussing what the companies *would* do for each other, which made it clear to me that the integration of the two companies hadn't happened yet.

When I met with the Canadian team at MAC, and subsequently with the Long Island team at Lauder, it was clear that they both bought into their marriage at the *worldview* level. Both companies were committed to broadening reach in the younger demographic and both were confident they had the products to do it.

However, the *standards* for how they would work together were not in sync. MAC described themselves as a "bad girl" company—fast moving, not tied down, edgy, breaking the rules. Lauder, on the other hand, prided itself on being the "good girl" company—dependable, sophisticated, delivering consistently year after year, and playing by the rules. The team at MAC felt unappreciated and, in some cases, trivialized for not being a long-standing brand with a world-class research team. The team at Lauder felt that MAC saw them as outdated and rule-bound. The Lauder team chafed at the idea MAC did not respect their years of experience and ground-breaking scientific innovations.

I could see these two groups were having a classic *chocolate conversation*.

The more I talked with the two different teams, the more I could see the common worldview. It was understood that MAC would bring relevance and new growth and Lauder would scale the brand globally and introduce cost-effective research practices which would improve productivity. Both teams shared and agreed with this worldview. This was the basis for the two companies coming together.

Things broke down when each company realized they had different standards for how they would bring products to market. They also had different work practices and compliance standards. Having the same worldview and being unable to deal with different standards led to frustration on both sides. This happens frequently when merged companies are as clear on the worldview as MAC and Estée Lauder were, wind up questioning the other's commitment to the shared cause, because the different standards come across as roadblocks, and people lose patience with each other.

So, what do you do when you reach this point? You do the same thing inside the organization you would do *outside* if you were having a Chocolate Conversation with your customers. You find out what's going on with people by talking to them and hearing their concerns. Remember, behind every concern is an unmet need. When you lead a company in this kind of situation your first priority is to uncover those unmet needs and figure out how to address them. Those unmet needs will tell you what part of the picture is missing or distorted in people's minds. You'll get all the clues you need to stop this *chocolate conversation* from going any further if you talk to people and find out what is really going on with them—and turn it into a Leadership Conversation.

We met with the head of MAC Research and key members of his team to better understand their operation, current practices, and business model. We then met with Shahan and the people on the R&D side of Estée Lauder. We documented our interviews and produced a themed synthesis we refer to as *"rapid insight."* These interviews uncovered the standards and concerns of both groups and provided the foundation for the work we needed to do with the teams.

We scheduled a two-day workshop with both teams during which we worked through the issues. We put together a "go forward plan" and a few well-focused actions to execute the plan. We put the team in cross-company pairs and had them read through the synthesis, point by point. We asked them to highlight what was hurting their progress and what could advance their progress if they each made some concessions. The most important part of this workshop was both teams coming together to understand their standards and figuring out what they were going to do about them—without sacrificing the value of MAC's "bad girl" image *or* Estée Lauder's "good girl" image.

That was 20 years ago, and, in a conversation with Shahan about a decade later, this is what he had to say:

> *"Our CEO hired former Proctor and Gamble VP Carl Haney to be Harvey's successor. He is working alongside Harvey and with me to eventually take over the operation. I brought him to MAC in Canada for a visit, and he was very impressed with their operation and integration into Estée Lauder. He saw how smoothly things were running, how well people from MAC, R&D, and Lauder were working together and bringing innovative*

products to market. He asked me what the secret to the success of this acquisition was over some of the others he's experienced. I told him these are the three big insights we uncovered and acted on as a result of our work with fassforward Consulting Group:

1. *The two brands are like two people who come together to form a relationship and become a couple. Each has their individual identities and personalities, and then there is the identity and personality of the couple. They needed to establish that third identity and personality without diminishing each other.*
2. *If they were willing to acknowledge and adopt the best of what both companies brought to the table, "all boats would lift."*
3. *Lastly, we recognized that we needed a well-respected Integration Manager who would be a liaison between the two brands. It took me a while to convince Harvey that this was a needed and viable full-time position that would more than pay for itself. It did."*

The first point—establishing a "third identity...without diminishing each other" is exactly where merger integrations go wrong. I see one company swallow another all the time. I also see companies limp along with different teams pulling in different directions because "legacy cultures" are still alive years after the merger. Creating a third identity is what gets you to "1 + 1 = 3." The third identity is what makes more out of the partners than just the two companies now appearing on the same P&L. Three things are needed in order to make this happen:

1. Get the people who shared a common worldview when they merged to talk about their cultural differences and address their standards head on. You can't let different standards simmer and turn into serious concerns.
2. Have teams collaborate together to identify and work through focused actions that will embrace each other's standards and help create the third identity.

3. Appoint an Integration Manager and give that person the resources they need to do the job.

As a note here, I have, in the past, seen some companies employ a full-time integration manager and a small, effective integration team with members drawn from key stakeholders across the company. These groups worked together productively for two years, which is a great investment in the future of the combined company. When you think of the cost of a failed merger, every dollar spent on these teams is a sound investment.

Always remember where the information comes from to make things work: Talk to your people. Listen to their concerns. Behind those concerns is the answer which will help you clear up confusion and get things back on track.

In the Estée Lauder acquisition of MAC, the companies found success through establishing a third identity for their union and the result is, they flourished. For other companies, it is not a third identity they need, rather a way to enhance each other's strengths while maintaining their unique identity and unique culture.

Let's look at Amazon's 2017 acquisition of Whole Foods, which was met with a lot of optimism. The deal allowed Amazon to grow beyond its notable e-commerce platform and sell groceries in hundreds of Whole Foods stores while also collecting significant shopper data. In the meantime, Whole Foods could lower its prices, a common gripe among shoppers. Whole Foods CEO John Mackey first described the partnership as "love at first sight." However, like many failed mergers, it was only a year later when there was no love lost between the two.

Their issues were predictable because the two companies may have seen value in capitalizing on each other's strengths, but where they failed was in investigating cultural compatibility before signing on the dotted line.

Amazon's culture is a tight one, which is in contrast to the culture at Whole Foods. Amazon's culture values the two traits of consistency and routine. They thrive through their efficient orderliness and reassuring predictability, making them less adaptable. On the flipside, Whole

Foods' culture is much more fluid and loosely structured. They are from the mindset of eschewing rules, encouraging new ideas, and valuing discretion. Whole Foods tends to be more open and creative, but also more disorganized. Whole Foods' Mackey was a visionary, collaborative leader who advocated for change and empowered workers. Amazon CEO Jeff Bezos is known to expect unwavering discipline from his workers, which personifies the tight leadership style.

An Unlikely Merger Inside of an Acquisition

While working with leadership teams in the Interpublic Group of Companies, I had the pleasure of meeting Howard Draft, the Chairman of Draft Direct Worldwide, and Laurence Boschetto, the former President and CEO. He is currently a Senior Advisor. Draft Direct Worldwide was a successful direct marketing company founded in 1978. Draft was later acquired by Interpublic Group of Companies in 2000 along with several other well-known agencies.

Howard and Laurence were contemplating a merger with another company in the Interpublic portfolio, Foote Cone and Belding (FCB). FCB was the world's third oldest advertising agency, dating back to 1873. Fax Cone, the "C" of FCB[4] had once said:

"Good advertising is always written from one person to another. When it is aimed at millions, it rarely moves anyone."

When I saw that on the wall in FCB's Chicago office, I thought: *This man would have understood how to turn a Chocolate Conversation into a Leadership Conversation. Leadership conversations* reframe the way people see the world and move them to action.

Howard and Laurence talked with my partner, Gavin and me about the new realities facing marketing and media companies in the digital

---

[4] "Fairfax M. Cone, 74, the Founder And Chairman of Ad Agency, Dies." *The New York Times*, 21 June 1977. *(https://www.nytimes.com/1977/06/21/archives/fairfax-m-cone-74-the-founder-and-chairman-of-ad-agency-dies.html)*

age. They continued that conversation with their clients. They dug into what was going on in the consumer world and asked how Draft could create something new and different.

Howard and Laurence realized their clients were really asking for an advertising company that could do more than the 30 second ad. They wanted a different kind of agency, one who would understand consumer behavior, brand identity, and the influence of social media. They also wanted to measure the return they were getting on their investment in advertising and promoting their brand. The two saw how Draft, a direct marketer who was consumer-focused, and FCB, an ad agency that understood and promoted brands, could bring together the right capabilities to achieve what they referred to as "a new breed of agency." The newly merged "DraftFCB" company had to be able to address the new realities of a digital age.

Clients were looking for a company that could handle both "above the line" and "below the line" campaigns. In advertising, "above the line" companies use media, which is broadcast and published to mass audiences, while "below the line" companies use media which is more narrowly focused, tailoring messages to a niche audience. Draft Worldwide was a successful "below the line" agency, while FCB was a master of "above the line" campaigns. Integrating both companies would give clients the key things they wanted.

This change involved addressing two big cultural norms: the "below/ above the line" distinction, and the walls between agency disciplines. *The merger that created the new DraftFCB was predicated on the idea that an agency could work in a much more collaborative and productive way with each other and with each other's clients.* It was possible to get far more involved in clients' businesses to the point of becoming a partner instead of a vendor.

Breaking down the divisions between Draft and FCB and between the disciplines in each company was critical to the success of the new model. Breaking down the walls between the disciplines in the clients' marketing functions was another big hurdle. Everyone had to buy-in to make this work—all while the two companies were merging. This was a *chocolate conversation* waiting to happen!

fassforward worked collaboratively with taskforce teams to develop the new business model, which became the *wheel,* and map out the strategy for making it happen. The wheel was a symbol of eliminating lines and fostering "round table" collaboration. It brought all the disciplines in the new DraftFCB together. The wheel was designed to "...bring together the art and the science of marketing."

We worked with a cross section of leaders to identify challenges in implementing this change. Integrating, and simultaneously redesigning, the new DraftFCB had to take place for 10,000 employees in 96 offices spread across six continents. We worked with Laurence and his senior team to develop a custom workshop that would take the wheel team design and new ways of working to every merged DraftFCB agency across the globe.

We built the Chocolate exercise into the wheel workshop. In this segment, we started by asking participants to conjure up the picture in their minds that appeared when they heard the word "chocolate." Next, we asked people to write on a post-It note the first image they thought of. After everyone wrote something down, we asked for volunteers to read their responses. People always smiled as they heard what others said. Through hundreds of these sessions over the years, I've heard responses that ranged from M&M's to gourmet Belgian chocolate, to a Chocolate Labrador.

As they shared results, people laughed at some of the associations made in the group. The next question we asked was the clincher: "...if a simple concept like "chocolate" can evoke so many interpretations, how did the group think something like the "wheel" would be interpreted by the ten thousand people who had to work together to make it happen?" This was a great icebreaker for these meetings, and it helped surface the standards and concerns quickly. Laurence was then able to address these concerns on the spot.

People around the globe started calling out a *chocolate conversation* when they heard one. It became code in the company for, "we are not on the same page." We heard people at all levels saying, "we're having a *chocolate conversation.*"

The wheel workshops were followed up by webinars, supporting materials on the company intranet site, with quarterly visits to support, and case studies to show proof points. All of this was implemented to translate the message in as many different ways as was needed to unbundle *chocolate conversations* and reinforce standards—and concerns.

The essence of what the company was doing was clear in all 96 offices. *AND*, the application was tailored to be relevant to the local markets. Laurence used the idea of the *chocolate conversation* in his presentations all over the world. It was amazing how different the standards for chocolate were in cities like New York, Chicago, Rio, Dubai, Johannesburg, Mumbai, and Shanghai.

After talking about Chocolate and Worldviews, Standards and Concerns in each of these geographies, DraftFCB people got it. Laurence understood cultural nuance and was not rigid about applying the U.S. standard for implementing the new model. In his words:

"You don't want to dumb it down, but you don't need an exact translation either. You are looking for the essence—a platform and philosophy for how we work that is balanced with what is appropriate to each region globally."

Laurence got *The Chocolate Conversation* when he first heard it, and the concept of it resonated across the globe. Everywhere we went, in multiple languages people were breaking down worldviews, standards, and concerns. We established global standards with local flavor.

I spoke with Laurence recently and discussed our experiences together, and he said:

"When you understand the subtleties of Chocolate, you get the dilemma that any company involved in a transformation faces. The nuance of language brings different views, and these views can undermine everything we are trying to do. Understanding standards and concerns and dealing with them right, at the outset are vital to successful change."

Within a year of the merger of Draft and FCB, Kmart switched its $740 million account from Grey New York to DraftFCB without a pitch, saying DraftFCB was uniquely qualified to meet their needs. That was back in April of 2007. In October 2008, Ad Age focused on the state of the agency two years after the merger, saying:

"In the two years since the Chicago-rooted agencies Draft and FCB merged, the agency has won more than 250 pieces of business around the globe, including Kmart, Qwest and the U.S. Census Bureau."

Ad Age later said that DraftFCB's merger was the only one in living memory which had resulted in a new business model that actually worked. People in other agencies began clamoring for DraftFCB's playbook.[1]

Though this is a great compliment to hear from peers, Laurence and Howard knew what we've seen several times in our conversation together. It's less about the playbook and more about the unique challenges you face, the way you talk with your people—inside and outside—to find the path which works for that unique set of issues. I come back to what Laurence said earlier: *"When you understand the nuances of Chocolate, you get the dilemma that any company needs to change."*

I have shared two examples from two very different companies who made change happen. Both companies had strong, committed leaders who understood change is never easy, that it happens in the conversation, and you have to be the one to lead people through it.

A recent example of an acquisition which worked through maintaining uniqueness is Amazon's acquisition of Zappos. In 2009, Amazon bought online shoe merchant Zappos for $1.2 billion. As a part of the deal, Amazon promised to leave Zappos alone so long as Zappos met financial targets. It was key to the deal for Zappos, as the companies formalized the arrangement in contract form. Zappos was proud of its unique identity: putting customers first with an engaged and happy workforce. Indeed, CEO Tony Hsieh published a bestselling novel in 2010 titled *Delivering Happiness*[5] that detailed his management style. While Zappos wanted Amazon's background one-click distribution, it did not want to lose what made it great when Amazon rolled in. It didn't have to. And the arrangement worked.

Whether a third identity is the answer or whether independent identities are the answer, you need to market how your union works, inside and out. Ensure your stakeholders understand it and appreciate it. Ensure a cross section of leaders are on board and can disseminate the message. Use workshops and webinars to keep employees informed, aware, and invested, and do not forget to provide quarterly updates and visits.

In families and companies alike, the people that comprise the whole should feel informed, involved, and heard. And they should believe in the future prospects of their union. These will help you to avoid the post-acquisition blues and to ensure long-term success.

---

[5] Hsieh, Tony. *Delivering Happiness.* Grand Central Publishing, Illustrated Edition, 19 Mar. 2013

Chapter Five

Addicted to Relevance

Growth, scale, and productivity have always been at the forefront of leaders' minds. Traditionally, corporate leaders will look for new ways to grow and take advantage of their scale. As we discussed in the previous chapter, if they aren't growing fast enough on their own, they will look to a merger or an acquisition to expedite growth. Many of these companies will take significant productivity measures to maintain profitability. This means cutbacks and reductions in force; commonly known as RIF's.

The big question—the one that *should* be keeping CEOs up at night, but seldom gets asked is *"are we relevant?"* Do customers want what we have? In reality, customers and shareholders will answer the question even if you're not asking it.

As in the case of Xerox and IBM, both CEOs recognized the products they were offering, once new and innovative, became a commodity or something customers no longer wanted or needed. Companies don't get growth without relevance. When companies are growing, they can take advantage of their scale and leverage productivity to achieve profitable growth.

When I think about the context of transforming any company, I think about what makes a startup take off. There really isn't a difference between the two: a new company or a company that is transforming. You need to start by offering people what they want and what they are willing to pay for. Those two aspects will tell you what's **relevant** to them.

For example, back in the 1950s and 60s, cars were it. Everyone who could drive wanted one and did whatever it took to get one. The automobile industry was a massively expanding market. With the advent of technology, we can see a progression from one new "have to have it!" to the next. In the 1980s, it was computers; in the 1990s, mp3 players; in the 2000s, smartphones and tablets. In the 2010s, and continuing, it is electric vehicles. In contrast, the mega-empires of the 1950s, like GM and Sears Roebuck—who didn't remain relevant—are on life support.

Businesses who are not relevant may hobble along but will eventually fail and may end up in receivership. The mere passage of time doesn't rob you of relevance. It's what you do when it's your time to do it. Alan Mulally revitalized Ford by saying:

> *"Everybody says you can't make money off small cars.*[6] *Well, you'd better damn well figure out how to make money because that's where the world is going."*

Mulally recognized, as did Steve Jobs, that companies need to anticipate consumer demand if they want to survive. The key to launching a business and then reinventing it time and again is an obsession with *relevance*—and that means change. Relevance is the catalyst for *growth*. This is a universal truth that stretches from political careers, to products, to services, to ideas.

Relevance is an idea or a product whose time has come. When someone hits on a political idea that is relevant to people, it spreads like wildfire and a person can become a national figure overnight. Look at how quickly the Occupy Wall Street movement grew into a nationwide phenomenon from a single demonstration in a cramped New York City Park. Remember how fast the Berlin Wall fell and Soviet authority vanished in Eastern Europe. The powerful USSR dissolved when the *idea* that things could really be different took hold. We all watched the

---

[6] Taylor III, Alex. *"Fixing Up Ford"*. CNN Money, 12 May 2009. *(https://money.cnn.com/2009/05/11/news)*

news as the Arab Spring turned into massive change in Tunisia, Egypt and Libya.

Now move it to business. Look at how quickly people embrace technologies they never knew they needed mere months before. Some of these innovations, like Google, Facebook, and YouTube, are ideas that connect people and content. Others, like the iPhone, are devices that provide an environment in which social networks like Facebook, Twitter, Instagram, and Snapchat happen. All of these relevant ideas have created new markets, disrupted old ones, and generated billions of dollars of growth. These sectors did not exist a decade ago.

Ford has made a strong comeback from its past woes. Facebook's IPO initially lost 30% of its value because investors questioned how it could be monetized. As of 2023, Facebook's stock is at 214.87. *Relevance doesn't just mean "new" or "digital"—it is what connects people to something they care about.*

The Great American Chocolate Conversation

On July 27, 2004, a young, passionate Senator from Illinois started a conversation with us at the Democratic National convention. We were intrigued. He captured our attention with his ideals and his candor. Whether we agreed with him or not, we listened and we heard something which stirred many of us. That resonance set the stage.

Four years later, on March 18, 2008, he had another conversation with us—a conversation about change titled "A More Perfect Union." He told us upfront it wasn't going to be easy, that we would face hardships and challenges. He made it clear that if we wanted to reclaim our relevance in the world, grow our economy through innovation and education, increase jobs and productivity, and scale our influence by building relations with our foreign neighbors, things had to change. We bought into the conversation—his worldview was our worldview, and whether he was our candidate of choice, we elected him to the highest office in our government. Barack Obama became President of the United States and leader of the free world. Why?

He was relevant to a broad audience. He used contemporary and conventional methods to reach us. Young people engaged in a conversation, most for the first time, with a soon-to-be global leader through social media, blogs, and Facebook. You could invite him to join your network on LinkedIn and he accepted. He bridged the generation gap. He was approachable to young people and credible to an older generation.

What he said mattered. He stayed on message and scaled that message across the globe. He brought people from all walks of life, genders, ethnicities, and ages to the conversation—and it wasn't a *chocolate conversation.*

Obama came with a worldview that resonated on a deep level for so many: jobs, change, integrity, growth, respect, and leadership. A country we could be proud of, showing up for family-by-family in increased value for all. His message was relevant. He was relevant.

What happened to that conversation eight years later? Did the people of our nation and of the world believe they were still in the same conversation with him? Did they believe they were in *any* conversation with him? People wanted his worldview played out according to their own standards, but it's not how it seemed to go. He stopped engaging with us and the result ended up being *chocolate conversations* everywhere.

What I'm saying has nothing to do with endorsing a presidential candidate, his policies or platform. What it has to do with is when people are left to think what they will about what is going on, it is natural for *chocolate conversations* to emerge. I'm talking about how a message which started out clear and engaging across a broad audience eventually deteriorated into *chocolate conversations* all over the nation.

Successful businesses experience the same sort of deterioration. You can find yourself in a *chocolate conversation* with your customers and your employees every bit as derailing as one in the political arena we just discussed. When you disappoint your customers and fail to meet their standards, they go elsewhere—*fast.*

Over forty years ago, a well-known retailer named Sears, Roebuck & Company told their customers through their advertisements that "*the customer is king.*" Customers believed their message because the salespeople in the stores delivered on that promise. The conversations Sears was having with their customers mirrored the conversation their employees were having. The worldview, *"the customer is king,"* translated throughout the company. Customers' standards were met so well that Sears was a household name and a revered brand. They were relevant, growing, and had national scale. The biggest retail presence in the country, Sears grew to where their revenues represented 2% of total US GNP.[2] What happened?

Wal-Mart came on the scene on July 2, 1962, and Sears scoffed at them. After all, they were *Sears.* As Wal-Mart offered better prices and an acceptable customer experience, Sears changed the conversation. The new focus was on profit and price point and the customer was no longer king.

Not long ago, I heard Sears mentioned on the radio and realized I hadn't thought about them in ages. They were contemplating selling off their Land's End subsidiary to bring in enough cash to keep going after years of decline in store traffic. They've gone nearly twenty years without turning a profit and have closed dozens of stores. They aren't relevant anymore.

Customers still buy what Sears sells. They just don't buy it from Sears anymore.

What "Addicted to Relevance" Means

I was having a conversation with a client about Steve Jobs a few years before Jobs passed away. The usual stuff came up, such as Steve's relentless focus on user experience, simplicity, and elegant design. My client asked me what I thought was the key ingredient to Jobs' success. I quickly replied, "He's addicted to relevance." That really grabbed my client's attention, and when I heard the words come out of my own mouth, I did a double take as well! It's what got me thinking about the significance of *relevance and why certain companies succeed and others don't.*

Relevance was what Steve Jobs was all about.

When Jobs returned to Apple after the NeXt venture in 1996, he believed the key to customer adoption was simplicity, ease of use, and beautiful design. He called Apple's developers together and asked what they were working on. He put a hold on all their projects and redirected them to work on four straightforward challenges: build the best possible consumer desktop and portable computer and do the same for a business—two products for two market segments. His strategy was simple—so basic that everyone could immediately get it, work on it, and succeed within the company.

Keep It Simple

Apple's late 1990s and early 2000s computers for both personal and business use dominated the market and for good reason. The message of *simple and elegant,* which was embedded in Jobs' conversation about Apple's strategy, carried over into the company's design solutions. It was the keystone of the marketing campaign. The conversation inside the company became the same conversation with customers. From strategy to design, to marketing, to sales, to service and customer experience— *simple and elegant* played all the way through. Even long after Steve Jobs' passing it remains a vital part of why Apple is the most relevant consumer brand today.

Simplicity is part of the consistent *feel* of Apple products. Hipness, an ergonomic sense, user-friendly, state-of-the-art, and edgy, quality, and sensitivity to what customers want, are standards that permeate everything with the Apple logo. The experience of anything Apple makes or does is consistent across the board. You sense it in iPhones, just as you could in the Macintosh nearly thirty years ago. Think of Apple computers, phones, music devices, and data storage and back-up capabilities through iCloud. Customers trust that Apple will meet their standards and exceed their expectations in anything they do. Relevance has always been what makes Apple, Apple...*It's the thing about a constantly changing company that has never changed.*

The 4 Considerations of Business

I remember Steve Jobs coming into Xerox in the early 1980s to look at our Alto PC which we had never launched in a commercially viable form. Jobs had this uncanny ability to see what people would want and need before *they* realized they had any need for a new technology. What made it work was that Jobs had a team of people who had the same worldview, standards, and concerns as he had.

As the Apple team talked, you could virtually *see* the lights going on above all their heads. There was no chocolate here—they all had the same idea at the same time and the picture of how to make it real was consistent among them.

Our Xerox team, on the other hand, was nothing but *chocolate conversations* about the new technologies. It's why we could never market our own technologies successfully ourselves. We couldn't figure out a clear message about what this technology was for or why you would want to part with a thousand dollars for it. Jobs could hear our *chocolate conversations* and recognize them for what they were. That's part of why his interest in buying Xerox quickly faded and he just bought the technology he needed instead.

Back when I talked about Xerox's desire to imitate Lou Gerstner, I made the point that you can't turn your company around by borrowing someone else's playbook. Steve Jobs had the same halo around him Gerstner had almost thirty years ago, so the urge to imitate him and turn your company into the next Apple is certainly there. But imitating Apple won't help you anymore than lifting Lou's notes helped us. We need to consider how relevance fits into the bigger picture, and translate how it fits into *your* picture.

We've sifted through the ingredients that make up a *chocolate conversation*, the worldviews, standards, and concerns, which are crucial to the way people see what needs to be done in any organization, and why those elements are important to every conversation. Now, we'll take a further cut at what all businesses need to do to grow. We'll prove the declaration I made at the beginning of this book—that everything to do with leadership and change happens in the conversation. And it happens in the context of what I refer to as the **Four Considerations of Business**:

4 Considerations of business

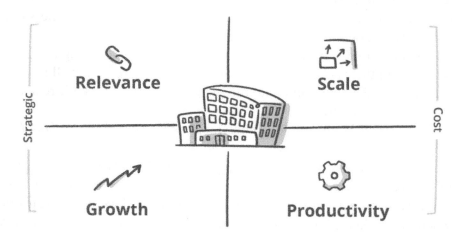

4 CONSIDERATIONS OF BUSINESS © 2021 *fassforward* Consulting Group

As I've said, many leaders haven't put "relevance" at the top of their list. When Allaire brought the consultants in to help turn our business around, the conversation and initiatives were all about productivity. I remember talking to Anne Mulcahy and saying, "Productivity is a code word for cutbacks." What's more, I knew that people weren't buying it. During the 2008 recession, I saw lots of companies putting in similar productivity measures. I've also seen companies spend millions to restructure their business in order to gain scale. Mergers and acquisitions are frequently driven by the desire to extend reach into new capabilities, geographies, and markets. Some companies, like International Paper, have "growth by acquisition" strategies—they just keep digesting more to fuel their own expansion in the marketplace.

Growth, scale, and productivity are all valid considerations of business; however, the strategies companies employ to achieve them breed *chocolate conversations* everywhere in the organization. And *chocolate conversations* can cost a company its relevance; people inside and outside the company lose track of the story. If what you do is not relevant to your employees, it won't be relevant to the customers they serve. If relevance *isn't* one of your business considerations, you'll find growth and scale difficult to achieve and productivity will be about shrinking your company.

Struggling With Relevance

I've spoken to groups of leaders over the past few years about Steve Jobs' addiction to relevance, and sometimes I get the reaction, "Well, if I launched a product like the iPhone, I'd have it made," or "Yes, but he just filled a really good niche." I don't think either of these observations is on target.

Things like this happen all the time in business. Someone sees a niche and fills it, and the market changes over time. The person who displaces you might not have been in the same industry last year, or even in business for very long.

Steve Jobs bet on user-friendly personal computers aimed at consumers wherever they might be. He didn't exhibit a bias towards businesspeople in an office, like everyone else did back then. This was part of the explosion of growth for Apple—you might think of it as a niche. Jobs gave consumers a PC which enabled them to start writing, banking, gaming, publishing, drawing, and designing—and this was before the internet linked all these activities to a wider world.

Jobs wasn't tied to one product line—this is an important point. You can dominate your market for years, only to find yourself pushed out because you've gotten too comfortable in your position. Jobs moved from computers to iPods and made Apple a player in the music world— before moving on to iPhones and iPads.

There was a time when Apple *never* would have gotten into music. Back in the 1970s, the Beatles objected to the name of the then new Apple Computer Corporation because the Fab Four's record label and umbrella organization for their businesses was called *Apple*. Jobs signed an agreement with the Beatles' Apple, allowing him to use the name because he was running a computer company that would never have any overlapping music or media interests—so there would be no confusion over the two companies' products.[3]

Then…Jobs looked at the Sony Walkman and he had another epiphany about something consumers could use that wasn't on the radar yet. The early Sony Walkman played cassettes and morphed later on to be a CD player. However, the Sony Walkman was limited in that it could play only an album's worth of material—maybe a dozen songs at best.

Jobs asked his designers, "…what if we could give people a thousand songs in digital quality in a device the size of a credit card? Why not carry your entire personal music library around with you everywhere you go?" This was the idea behind the iPod. After introducing the iPod in October 2004, Apple dominated the digital music player sales market in the United States, capturing 90% of the market for mp3 players and over 70% of the market for all types of portable players. In the first quarter of 2008, iPod sales accounted for 42% of Apple's revenue, followed by 21% from laptop computer sales and 16% from PC sales. At the time, these were significant numbers. Since then, and in the third quarter of fiscal year 2019, Apple generated 48.29 percent of its revenue from iPhone sales. Since its introduction in 2007, Apple's iPhone sales have consistently increased, going from around 40 million units sold in 2010 to about 218 million iPhones sold in 2018 alone. Apple Shipped an estimated 36.4 million iPhones worldwide in the first quarter of 2019, and sales of Apple's AirPods nearly doubled to $6 billion this year— and will likely take another leap forward next year—according to Toni Sacconaghi of Bernstein. The analyst noted that Apple could sell 85 million AirPods in 2020, generating about $15 billion in revenue. They actually sold 108.9 million!

Stop for a moment and consider how long IBM stayed married to the mainframe business. Mainframes were the cash cow for the company for 20 years, and they were the platform for building the solutions business that was the bedrock of IBM's next period of growth. IBM actually withheld new technologies from the market, sometimes for a few years, to let service contracts on existing products run their course.

Apple is different—the company is completely willing to replace innovative products that still have life in them if there are new ideas and products which can change customers' lives. In other words, Apple is willing to cannibalize its own niche markets to launch something new and exciting, effectively staying ahead of the curve on…you guessed it…relevance.

Not satisfied with having just a strong home PC market, Apple went on to launch iBooks, then iPods, then iPhones, then iPads, then iCloud and AirPods—all in pursuit of customers' collective tomorrows. Look at the future as Apple sees it: the company expected iCloud to become the backbone of their revenue in the coming decade, moving the business from devices to online storage capacity and online environments. And in early 2020, reports indicated that Apple's revenue from AirPods exceeded that of Spotify, Twitter, Snapchat, and Shopify combined.

So, what's going on in this company? Is it that they've had the luck to hit on killer products several times in a row? I don't think that's the story at all. Jobs' relentless addiction to relevance, *and* his insistence that the company itself stays relevant is the core worldview of Apple.

This is a company that seems to have very few Chocolate Conversations. There is a real line of sight from worldviews to standards. Apple people get the message, and that message carries through to their customers. Apple users are simply not interested in hearing what other computer companies have to say. Apple speaks directly to them—to the worldview and standards *they* have as end users.

Back in May 2012, according to Britain's Millward Brown Optimor's study of the Top 100 Brands in the world, Apple was the number one most valuable brand in the world—at $183 Billion, superseding number 2, IBM at $115 Billion. At the end of 2019, seven years later, Forbes ranked Apple as number one at $205.5 Billion with Google in a distant second at $167.7 Billion. It's hard to call such a huge business a niche company—but if Apple has a niche at all, it isn't in products, it's in *relevance itself.*

What's critical about being addicted to relevance is you don't even need to make a product. Think about YouTube. This platform started as a file-sharing protocol that a few people put together so they could exchange videos online. Only a few years later, it had become so universal that Google bought it from its developers for a billion and a half dollars. YouTube has completely changed the face of online music and video. It's grown to be one of the primary ways in which new music and video artists become known as well as a way for people to demonstrate everything from how-to-videos to travel logs.

Marketing for traditional feature films is changing rapidly because of YouTube. The 2012 blockbuster Ridley Scott film, *Prometheus,* put up advertising for the android featured in the film—marketing a product the film imagines will be available in about 80 years! *Prometheus'* viral marketing generated enormous buzz even though the plot of the film was a closely guarded secret.

LinkedIn, Twitter, and Facebook are additional examples of another idea people never knew they needed. The spread of social media from college campuses to—well, pretty much—*everywhere* in the past decade is changing how people interact, get jobs, sell *anything*, represent themselves and meet potential spouses.

Yet, we keep getting pulled back to earth by practical concerns. Part of Facebook's ethos has always been *quality of the experience over commerce.* The site was developed with the quality of the user experience paramount and commercial concerns put off to the side. When I wrote my first book, General Motors pulled a $10 million advertising account from Facebook right before the IPO, and the offering itself was rocky. Facebook stock dropped from the opening price of $38 a share into the mid $20s. At the time, the big question was, can you keep the flavor of Facebook and still sell advertising space? Is conventional advertising relevant to Facebook users? It remained to be seen, and no one could doubt the company's relevance as a social site, even as they scrambled to make their IPO worth the money.

Since writing *The Chocolate Conversation*, the numbers have been impressive, to say the least. As of January 2020, they have 2.5 billion monthly active users, and 1.6 billion daily users with five new profiles created every second. Think about that—over two human beings in six are involved in Facebook. Add to that, there was a time when people couldn't figure out how to monetize it. According to the State of Inbound Marketing (2012) 42% of marketers report that Facebook is critical to their marketing plans for their businesses, and 16 million local business pages have been created since May 2013, a 100% increase from 8 million the previous year. Long story short, Facebook figured out a way to monetize. Oh, and its stock price is now over $200!

You can be relevant and be a more traditional business that does well in both brick and mortar and digital worlds. Barnes & Noble was a great example of this. Many bookstore chains, notably Borders, folded in the past several years because they had not been able to compete with stores like Amazon and the eBook phenomenon. People don't want to take the time to visit the store when it's just too easy to get online, and your purchase will arrive the very next day. Barnes & Noble has revamped its retail stores with amenities like Internet cafes, and Starbucks coffee kiosks, making the reading experience more pleasant, and having more staying power than simply visiting racks of the store.

At the same time, their website is well put together. It is cross-referenced well, and fulfillment is exemplary—clearly the company has put a lot of effort into making sure the feel of the website reflects the same flavor as the stores. By moving into the online environment without fear, and maintaining its flavor, both virtually and in the stores,

Barnes & Noble has ensured its ongoing relevance while many of its competitors have failed.

As for loss of relevance, the American record industry is a perfect example of a once huge business that never saw change coming. Pre-recorded music was an almost *"can't go wrong"* bet in the 1960s and 1970s. Companies like Warner Communications were making billions in the glamorous rock-and-roll and disco worlds.

And then Napster appeared. Its revolutionary file-sharing technology has virtually destroyed the pre-recorded music industry. Now, all the young people I know stream songs and videos from iTunes and Apple Music on their smartphones without much concern about who the copyright owners are, or whether they are paying for music or not.

Record labels have lost relevance with consumers. Digital music made it possible for iPhone and Apple Music—which runs $9.99 per month for an individual account, or $14.99 per month for a family of up to six people (which requires iCloud Family Sharing). College students can subscribe for only $4.99 per month. This generates billions of dollars in revenue for Apple and creates hundreds of millions of delighted consumers. The pre-recorded music industry doesn't seem to be able to figure out how to plug into this consistently growing market. Instead, the industry is locked in acrimonious arguments with its own artists and customers, many of whom cannot see why they even need record labels anymore. Not surprisingly, the industry has been shrinking sharply every year since the late 1990s.

The Curse of Success: Why Kodak Doesn't Own Digital Photography

Long term success is a paradox—it's what everyone is looking for—but it is also a place where many companies are tempted to stop having active conversations with their customers.

Take Kodak, for example. In 1976, Kodak had a 90% share of the US photo film market. It had been a titan for decades. So, where is Kodak today?

Kodak sharply underestimated the competition it would face from computer printers, cell phones and the Internet. None of these seemed to be in the same market segment—yet these were the very ingredients that have linked together to absorb America's love of photos.

In the 70s and early 80s, it was unlikely that anyone other than a futurist would have dreamed of a threat from early PCs and dot matrix printers. However, by the 90s, high quality printers and digital formats were beginning to eat into Kodak's photo paper sales, and the first digital cameras were appearing. As a sign of the times—and one that Kodak should have taken note of—Dell used to give away early digital cameras with their desktop computer/monitor/printer packages. These digital cameras were so cumbersome, they could only hold 50 or so pictures in memory, and they ate through batteries in just a few hours of use. But consumers loved them—and, if Kodak had been engaged in active conversation with their customers, they would have seen the opportunity.

There was a strong desire for the immediacy and control of digital pictures coupled with the speed and versatility Kodak products offered. Unfortunately for them, Kodak focused only on its core business, unwilling to incubate a digital arm which would eventually supplant the huge cash cow film and paper business. Kodak focused instead on preloaded film/camera packages, a new version of an old concept dating all the way back to George Eastman's day.

Kodak ended up being late to the digital photography scene and paid the price. It hasn't turned a profit since 2007, it went bankrupt at the end of 2011, and, in early 2012, Kodak announced it was abandoning consumer digital cameras to focus on corporate imaging. The company had already abandoned selling traditional film cameras.[6]

You can look back to 1976 and it's hard to understand why Kodak failed to stay with the trends and become the biggest digital photography powerhouse of the present. Follow the story forward, however, and you see that *consumer standards changed*. Kodak was not following the conversation closely and they missed the whole shift. Their stock price dropped dramatically from the 80s, where it sold in the $70 to $100 per share range, to the early 2000s, where it has remained under $10 per share, and there is no sign indicating Kodak will recover.

The worldview for consumers and Kodak both stayed the same—affordable, quality photos for the average non-expert consumer. The standards switched to digital speed and ability to control the image, and Kodak missed more than the boat. By missing that vital shift, the ocean liner has long ago sailed without them. They became irrelevant—another analog casualty of a digital age. The *chocolate conversation* they had with their customers cost them the whole company.

Staying in the Conversation with Your Customers

Consider the rise of Amazon, especially during Covid-19's sheltering in place. Jeff Bezos, Amazon's former CEO, is currently the richest person in the world; and Amazon is the third largest company in the U.S. by market capitalization. Amazon dominated online commerce in recent years, but now the company is essential to the consumer market. During the days of social distancing, households turned to online delivery as the primary means of shopping. What's most notable is how Amazon has been able to respond effectively to the exponential increase in demand. (Note that other companies are also rising to the challenge of the current times. You will know who they are if you look at your own habits, such as Chewy, Instacart, and Uber Eats.) While its distribution channels were in place before Covid 19, Amazon adapted swiftly to the heightened demands. And where it cannot meet prior expectations on deliverables, the company has successfully communicated such challenges to consumers. Will consumer habits remain changed so that Amazon continues to remain not only relevant, but essential,even now, after the pandemic? While it remains to be seen, the number of Amazon Prime trucks spotted in neighborhoods across America supports an answer in the affirmative. So how do you stay in the conversation with consumers and keep your relevance? For one thing, don't get comfortable no matter *how* successful you are. Businesses today can't—and won't—stand still. The only constant we face in business today is change itself.

As another example, look at what Richard Branson has done with Virgin to stay relevant and keep growing. Virgin began as a record store in the early 1970s—just *one* record store. By the end of the 70s, it was a major record label. Recorded music grew at a strong pace from the mid-60s to the mid-80s and was glamorous—and, unlike the movie industry, records were inexpensive enough to make that you could actually get into the industry if you had a couple of bands that caught on.

Branson's real genius was in consumer conversations. Every time he saw customers in *any* business walk away disappointed, Branson imagined how he would have handled the situation. When he saw consumer demand for reasonable ticket prices in the deregulation of the airline industry, Branson and his record company launched an airline, Virgin Atlantic, in the 1980s—hardly a move other entertainment companies would have considered.

In the same decade, Branson sold his smaller-record retail outlets and launched Virgin Megastores to capitalize on the consumer's desire for the rich shopping experience he felt was poorly served. In 1992, he sold the Virgin Records business to EMI—he actually sold the most glamorous, oldest, and seemingly most lucrative part of the company. He told the press he had tears in his eyes as he signed away what many thought was the heart of his business.

This turned out to be a tremendously far-sighted move. EMI paid the highest price for a record company acquisition ever negotiated to-date. A couple of years later, the advent of file-sharing I referenced previously caused an implosion in the record industry, while Branson's Virgin Group is now a venture capital conglomerate of over 400 companies with global interests in consumer products, transportation, and entertainment.[7]

The one constant ingredient which has made Branson a billionaire and Virgin a household name is a profound capacity for reinvention —while simultaneously retaining a cache of "hip" and "customer-friendly" that is part of Branson's DNA. Branson knows how to have a conversation with customers—and he's so good at it, it doesn't matter *what* business he's in.

The level of change at Virgin over the years might verge on the ridiculous—a bit like Hewlett-Packard abandoning the computer printer business or Kodak giving up on cameras. However, think about where Virgin is today, compared to a company like Kodak.

Here's the bottom line: you can radically transform your company like a Richard Branson, or you can let the market do it for you as Kodak did. No matter what you do or don't do, and no matter how big and seemingly secure you are today, change *will* happen. You have to be able to guide that change yourself. If you are passive about what is happening to you, you'll become irrelevant, you'll be humiliated by how fast you'll shrink, and you'll become just another footnote instead of one of the main players.

How to Find Your Relevance

The Covid-19 pandemic has been a strange new reality we have lived through. Businesses across the globe faced time crunches to stay relevant in their industry. When we eventually came out of the corona hibernation, who opened their doors for business and whose doors will remain shuttered for good? Companies large and small have asked this question and are doing what they can to avoid being one of the casualties of Covid 19. They have to think fast, and strategically, about how to reshape their business model to meet market and societal changes. Now, more than ever, they need to focus on the key ingredient to success... especially at this time in history.

While society was holed up in their homes during the global pandemic, consumer demands shifted dramatically. Businesses across industries are facing direct or indirect fallout from those demand shifts. Everyone is impacted and no one can afford to stay static. What are you doing to ensure your product or service is and will be in demand in the coming weeks, months, and years? What are you doing to ensure you will remain relevant to the marketplace?

We've talked about why relevance is so important as a business consideration. So how do you do it?

Market leaders have to ask:

* Are we relevant?
* Do our customers want what we have?
* Are we listening to them?
* Do we know what problems our customers have, and can we provide a solution?
* Do we need to change our business model?
* Are we easy to do business with—and if not, why not, and how
* can we fix it?
* Do our employees know:
    * Who we are?
    * What we do?
    * Why customers choose us?

When you can answer these questions and address the issues that will surface, you can begin a path forward which will lead to renewed relevance and growth. I'll conclude this part of our conversation by emphasizing how closely knit relevance and growth are. Many successful small companies find out what's missing from the offerings of big companies and then find a way to be relevant in these niches. Their relevance creates a market and fuels their growth—like Jobs did with Apple, they create new markets in spaces that are under-served or completely overlooked.

Put it this way: scale and productivity issues are high-class problems when you are relevant and growing. Without relevance and growth, you have an anchor dragging your company down. Put your attention where it needs to be—get addicted to relevance.

Chapter Six

Why do Good People have Bad Conversations?

People follow leaders. They listen to their leaders and act accordingly. That is why you will hear me say that *Leadership Happens in the Conversation*—I've said this so many times, it could be considered a mantra for me and for my clients. If so, why is it well respected leaders can have conversations which cause more harm than good?

There were powerful real-life events happening at the time of writing this book. In March 2020, we all became acutely aware of the Coronavirus and its global and national impact. Escalating each day, the scientists' numbers were frightening. Early projections out of the United Kingdom indicated the death count in the millions, creating a ripple effect of fear and panic. The virus was known to be highly contagious, there was no vaccine for it, and it tended to target and weaken the elderly and those with compromised immune systems. The initial and only immediate antidote was to shut everything down and cradle the country. Before we knew it, seemingly overnight, companies that could, set up their employees to work from home. Children were schooled from home via Zoom (whose stock has done quite well as a result), anyone in the service industry scrambled to file their unemployment claims and healthcare workers, and truck drivers, and grocers were now labeled "essential employees" (because they are, the term just hadn't been universal until now). During a spring when everything should have been blooming—the annual time of rebirth, the focus was on death and shutting down.

Rarely has it been so imperative to get a *Chocolate Conversation* right, yet it failed as a Leadership Conversation on so many levels.

Don't wear a mask. Wear a mask.

Don't touch anything. It doesn't live long on surfaces. Don't breathe near anyone.

The only consistent advice was to wash your hands for twenty-seconds and to social distance at six feet apart.

The confusion grew, as did the judgment of others who fell on one side or the other of the conversation—all led by the actions and inactions of our leaders from the top, down to the cities and towns.

On the surface, it seems leaders, businesses, and the people as a whole had the same worldview; health and safety come first. However, the conversation revolved around a proverbial "rock and a hard place." Here we have two major issues at stake. Keeping it on a national scale, we have a country that was experiencing a pandemic that has threatened our health and our lives. On the other hand, the economic toll on businesses, especially the mom-and-pop restaurants (as one example), has been catastrophic. Heading into summertime, seasonal locations that depend on six months a year of business to fuel them for the entire year were told there would be no economic season. The country was closed; come back next year, if all goes well.

A completely dispassionate observer might conclude the two sides (health and livelihood) are so intertwined in their worldviews that a little discussion over specifics *(standards)* should address their *concerns* and serve to solve both sides of the coin.

However, at a worldview level, the healthcare problems trump business, and livelihood forsakes the success of business. Although it appears everyone wants the same thing—to save lives—business owners found themselves trapped between saving their dreams and livelihood, putting food on their families' tables, and trying not to come across as self-serving.

While almost every President of the United States has spear-headed national and global crises, from pandemics to social injustices, from war and peace talks—none of them have been successful in doing it perfectly.

Our first challenge as a nation and globally is to determine at which level disagreement occurs. Survival issues, and health and business challenges can cause people to become desperate, or even violent, if they feel challenged beyond their tolerance.

There are plenty of examples in every sphere of life. For politicians, issues like Social Security, social justice, and healthcare are battlegrounds for powerful constituencies who have different worldviews. These differences paralyze genuine open debate. Members of Congress might not say so, but I sense they approach issues like these with a "win/lose" attitude. In spite of the fact they are members of a body entrusted to make the best decisions for the entire nation; in reality, they only pull from their point of view to the exclusion of the opposing point of view. This is what has polarized the political debate in our country for years now.

Prior to the pandemic, business leaders faced the same problems. They grappled with issues like spiraling pension liabilities and runaway healthcare costs. These issues are topics in union negotiations where *chocolate conversations* go on for weeks and months or sometimes longer. Rarely does an effective leadership conversation occur in these instances. Both parties recognize rising costs are forcing changes in employee benefits. Employees realize everything costs more. It's a double-edged sword. Rising costs support the rationale that companies can't afford to contribute more to employee benefits, yet the companies' very survival is at stake if they don't make cuts somewhere. To further exacerbate the debate, executive bonuses can be so high in those very same companies it seems like an easy fix is to use the bonuses to even out the gap. Most of the executives who get those bonuses don't want to consider that option, even during the pandemic. However, several did respond to the seriousness of the pandemic by forfeiting their salaries, such as: Marriott's CEO, Anthony Capuano, Ed Bastian of Delta as well as CEO Oscar Munoz and President Scott Kirby of United, H. Lawrence

Culp, Jr. the CEO of GE, Lyft's co-founders, Airbnb executives, and Bob Iger, Disney's Executive Chairman.

We have all witnessed large and small businesses reducing their workforce to accommodate rising costs. In these cases, the outcome is people losing their jobs, and the ones left behind having to do more with less. These problems aren't going away. Unions are fighting to survive in a pay-as-you-go economy, employees are fighting to keep their jobs, and companies are fighting to stay in business.

So, why can't smart people get in a room, have tough conversations, and work out a viable solution? Doing so requires each party to agree on a common worldview and establish new standards everyone can live by. That said, we must have a common worldview around what everyone keeps stating is the "new normal." This also means we must have new standards, because concerns that existed prior to the pandemic may no longer be at the forefront.

For another example of change happening on a global level, simply look at the Economic Forum in Davos, Switzerland. In 2020 the world's leaders discussed conscious capitalism in regard to stakeholder value versus shareholder value. Only one year later, the discussion was on the Great Reset. They discussed a whole New World Order around the environment and government. Some of the issues they addressed were climate change, how to deal with pandemics, the distribution of wealth, access to capital, and the monopoly of large businesses such as Amazon, Apple, Google, etc.

Whether in Davos, New York, DC, the UK, or anywhere else, leaders have to break through the stalemate by pushing through the mutually exclusive, "you win, I lose" scenario, to where everyone can make a contribution.

What You Say and How You Say It Matters

As we've talked about in earlier chapters, the biggest problem arises when people think they have communicated, but the message hasn't made it through. The gulf widens when what you expect and what other people think you want are different. How many times have you sent out a detailed communication only to get blank stares when you bring up topics you thought were clear?

Your employees would probably be just as baffled as you are if they realized they had missed something important. The problem is you might not have given people the chance to really hear you. I've read dozens of books and articles on communication that talk about a "waterfall of messages." The premise is, if you get your message positioned in the right channels, it will flow downstream giving everyone what they need to know. I love the watery image, but the waterfall idea is a myth. Something certainly flows downstream, but it isn't what was intended.

Corporate communication problems that lack *leadership conversations* are more like the children's game of "telephone," where one player whispers something to a second player, who whispers it to a third, and so on down the line until the last player reports what they heard. Everyone laughs because the message is ridiculously mangled by the time it gets to the end. Many adults are unaware of how frequently they continue to play this game in their business lives and how hard it is to stop. The key is to see what happens in people's minds as they translate what they think they've heard.

Media companies are really good at this. They translate what they know or sense that the customer wants and capture it into a slogan or a 30-second visual that depicts a feeling or a universal mood. Remember that Wendy's campaign, when a little old lady asked, *"Where's the beef?"* It's one thing to say, "Gee, our hamburgers are really a lot better than Burger King or McDonalds." It's another to come right out and say, "They don't deliver—we do" in a way so simple and memorable that it becomes an icon. You get it right away. It makes you laugh. It sticks. Mastercard's priceless campaign does the same thing. Everything you can buy with the card costs a little money here and a little money there, but the experience is *priceless. They have since transitioned to the message, "Doing well by doing good is business as usual," which speaks to the idea of making commercially sustainable social impact the new paradigm for business as usual. As a result, their concept of inclusive growth helps people who don't have access to cash by supplying them with cards. Through these cards, they can show their identity and participate in the economy.*

Verizon's early campaign *"Can you hear me now?"* is another one. Yes, it says "our network offers better coverage than theirs," but it says it in a way that gets to the heart of what we want from our cell phone service. The premise is basic, we want to hear the person on the other end of the phone wherever we are.

Verizon has since updated their campaign to include a more contemporary message of "we're ready for business," which during the pandemic where businesses had to reinvent the way they work, is timely. Verizon has also acquired the company BlueJeans in order to provide a Zoom-like experience.

Dunkin Donuts was taking a hit when Starbucks and other upscale, "cool" coffee spots came into existence. When the economy took a turn for the worse, Dunkin turned to Hill Holiday to help them get back their customers and attract new ones. Without saying their coffee was less expensive—and actually tastier than the upscale coffees, they positioned themselves as the company America wants in these trying times—good coffee at a fair price, without the hoopla. The message, *"America runs on Dunkin"* distilled a message people of all ages could relate to while providing a message of unity.

In each of these cases, people get it. It enters common speech and popular culture. It does what *you* are trying to do as a leader—help your people get the picture immediately from simple, clear language.

Something very clever is going on here, and leaders can learn a lot about effective communication and conversation from it. Wendy's, Verizon, Mastercard, and Dunkin are all consciously creating standards in the minds of millions of customers. We've talked about worldviews, standards, and concerns throughout this book, but let's spell them out again quickly with these media examples fresh in our minds. Remember that:

- Worldviews are the beliefs which we hold about ourselves, others, and the world itself, based on our experiences. They shape the picture of reality we each carry around in our heads.
- Standards are the guidelines we have in our heads that help us know how to act and evaluate what we see.
- Concerns are the results of the filtering job we perform with our worldviews and standards. Standards are expectations and the principals we live by. When those standards are not met, a concern will arise.

The common element in the media marketing messages is a clear link to a worldview—a good customer experience—and a product that delivers in a way that links right to the worldview. The listener feels that Wendy's concerns are their concerns. They can see themselves in the Mastercard commercials, having those *"priceless"* experiences. When they pick up their morning coffee and doughnuts at Dunkin, they feel as though they are part of a community. They've called Verizon after saying, "Can you hear me now?" one too many times while standing on their tiptoes or holding the phone near a window.

Throughout our time together in this book, I've been talking about how important it is to have your people see themselves in the change that has to happen in your company. Every one of these advertising campaigns is doing that very thing. Each is saying, "Change your consumer behavior and make me your preferred provider because I offer the experience *you WANT*."

This is the same task you face as a leader: You are trying to get people to change their behavior and make the company you all work for their preferred provider. By aligning with your customer, the company becomes "their" company—and you want them to see what's in it for them so we can transform "our" company.

Let's think about how these companies came to these ideas. While the marketing ideas seem simplistic in nature, I assure you, they did this carefully, because they had to be able to deliver on these promises. Like the Energizer Bunny—another great campaign—these companies had to live up to the standards they set, and they had to keep going and going and going. When you reach out to your customers at this level, this piece has to be the outward part of a conversation you are having with them. The beauty is people on the inside are hearing what your customers are hearing and everyone is on the same page.

The Inside Conversation Ought to Mirror the Outside Conversation

When our firm started working with Verizon Wireless, their network message," Can you hear me now?" was the rallying cry throughout the organization at all levels. Leaders, through to frontline employees, beamed with pride that their company was the preferred carrier who delivered on their promise every day.

I remember having an interview with the Chief Technology Officer. I asked him what was top of mind for him as a leader in his position. His response caught me off guard. I am rarely surprised by a leader's response, but this one stuck with me. He said, "Every day, I wake up in the morning with one focus: We have to deliver on the promise of our advertising."

That impressed me. Here was a leader who was bringing the conversation the company was having with its customers to his engineers every day.

Here's a story I heard second-hand while working with media firms in a large marketing communication holding firm:

A number of years ago, UPS invited a group of advertising executives to their office to discuss a new advertising campaign for the company. The various pitches from the ad folks were all falling flat on the assembled UPS senior leaders. Pitch after pitch landed to silence in the room until one of the UPS leaders got tired of it all. He demanded to know why the ad people weren't coming up with anything which captured the essence of UPS. "What are we supposed to do?" one of the ad people said, "You're a brown company." "Oh really?" the UPS leader shot back. "Well, let me tell you what this brown company can do for you!"

He passionately laid out what UPS was really about: the strong identity, the commitment to quality, being dependable to customers, a strong sense of accountability, and a lot of pride—right down to the distinctive *brown* trucks. His colleagues were as engaged as he was, nodding and leaning into the presentation; they were in the conversation with him as if they were all one. At the end, they collectively leaned across the table as the UPS leader slapped his hand on the table for emphasis and shouted, "And that's what brown can do for you!"

The ad agency people had the good sense to realize they had just heard an authentic, passionate message from the entire "inside" of UPS, voiced through its equally committed and passionate leader. This was the conversation they could and should have with customers on the outside. *"What can brown do for you?"* is yet another iconic message, intimately tied to the conversation within the company. Inherent in the slogan was the core message: Here we are, an everyday business, comprised of everyday people doing an extraordinary job for you anywhere in the world.

A savvy media company executive once told me a successful marketing message is nothing more than "An obvious message expressed in a simple way." That is *exactly* what you need to do as a leader—and it's hard. Leaders are faced with translating complex concepts into tangible and doable actions. The simpler the language and the shorter the message, the easier it is for people to understand and not misinterpret. This takes time and effort.

There are different conversations leaders need to have to convey their messages. We've broken them down into seven types of conversations:

1. Drive performance
2. Sell an idea
3. Change someone's mind
4. Share information
5. Resolve a problem
6. Recognize performance
7. Correct performance

There is a framework we use with our clients which helps to identify the type of conversation you want to have, and how to prepare to have it. It's "the Intention /Impact Loop," a 5-step method:

- The first step is to clearly understand your *Intention*: What you want to get across.
- The second step is to determine the *Investment* in time and resources you need to achieve your desired outcome.
- The third step is to determine the best way to have the *Interaction*: public presentation, small groups, webinar, email, one-on-one, or phone call.
- The fourth step is to consider how your audience will *Interpret* your message.
- The fifth and final step is to seek to understand the *Impact* your message has when it reaches the receiver.

You control the first three steps and can only influence the last two. The last two are crucial. Let's look at two examples of conversations through this framework:

I was once asked to "onboard" a new leader who reported to the Chief Operating Officer of the Company. He inherited a business which was under-performing—one of his biggest districts ranked at the bottom. The manager of the district was never around when he reached out to him. The leader was becoming more frustrated as time went on—he never left work before 9:00 P.M., and could not understand what he perceived as a total lack of urgency on the part of his district manager. One evening, our new leader got home around eleven and went directly to bed. He was dog-tired from a rough day. He woke up around 2:00 A.M., frustrated and angry, and fired off an email to this district manager. The following day, the district manager forwarded the email to the CEO of the company, asking if this was the kind of communication "leadership" should be sending at two o'clock in the morning? The DM asked if the tone, language, and overall message were in keeping with the company's values, which he listed. He went on to say his wife was having a difficult pregnancy, and he needed to pick up their son from school at 3:00 each day and drop him home. He couldn't work late, as he needed to be home to feed his son and get him to bed so his wife could rest. He acknowledged the performance of his district was suffering.

The intention of the email was to communicate a concern and get this DM back on track. I took this new leader through the Intention-Impact Loop and asked some questions: *Given your **intention**—how much time did you **invest** in considering what method of **Interaction** would best suit the situation? Did you consider how your DM would **interpret** your email? Did you think your email would achieve your desired outcome? What **impact** did your email have on your DM and ultimately on you?*

This new leader learned a painful lesson, that a simple pause before he hit the send button could have prevented the DM's response to the email. The criticality of the performance challenge warranted a face to face with this DM. This conversation would have uncovered the worldviews, standards, and concerns of both parties. This leader, with the help of his human resource partner, granted the district manager a family leave-of-absence and put a high-potential candidate in the interim position, until he returned to work. Performance improved and everyone got what they needed.

The second example is short and effective. We work with a high energy, smart human resource executive, Martha Delehanty, currently the CHRO for Commvault and previously the head of HR for Verizon Enterprise Solutions. Both positions at Verizon and Commvault require long hours and countless meetings since both are global companies. She and her HR leadership team work 24/7 with their business leaders to provide the counsel, talent, and development required to drive performance.

It is difficult for Martha to touch everyone in the global organization as often as she would like. One day, I was sitting in a meeting when I noticed a young HR associate director smiling as she was reading something on her phone. At the break, I heard her telling a colleague about a text message she received from Martha. She had participated on a task force that solved a problem for the business. The text simply said, *"You Rock!"* This employee was excited to receive such a thoughtful text from the Senior Vice President of HR. She felt special and acknowledged it—and it showed.

Martha's *intention* was to recognize this employee and praise her performance. The *investment* in time was minimal, and the method to have this *interaction* was timely, contemporary, and spot on. There was only one way for this employee to *interpret* Martha's message—the *impact* was powerful.

Many leaders complain about the lack of time they have to interact with their teams through to their frontline employees. I ask you to consider that sometimes a simple message, delivered in a simple way, can accomplish more than a long email, conference call, or face-to-face meeting.

Management by Meetings

Most companies try to get messages through by calling meetings. I've suffered through my share of them, as I'm sure you have. These meetings are usually accompanied by several PowerPoint decks which took people hours to prepare. These days, even after the pandemic restrictions, we are all suffering from Zoom fatigue!

Meetings that used to take up 60% of our time are now taking up 100% of our time and the 10% we reserve for our families. Meetings are used for communicating, setting direction, evaluating alternatives, course correcting, and reporting results. A lot of executives we work with are up to their eyebrows in meetings. There is the weekly staff meeting followed several days later by the weekly conference call, soon to be updated in the monthly operations review. There are meetings to prepare for executive reviews and board meetings.

Management by meetings makes it almost impossible to get things done and to move messages through the organization. *People spend more time describing the work than actually doing it.* I work with clients who literally spend the first half of the year preparing deckware and going to meetings. People get so bogged down in minutia that decision-making slows to a crawl. In a surprisingly large number of meetings, the attitude is punitive; people are put on the defensive and just try to make it through without being called out or getting more action items.

When companies are not performing, the tendency is to have more reviews. These reviews tend to negatively impact performance. The more time leaders spend in meetings, the less time they have to work with their teams, solve problems, see customers, and drive performance. The emphasis shifts from an external focus on customers and market leadership to an internal focus on metrics and financials.

Alan Mulally, when hired as the new CEO, said after one week at Ford Motor Company, "You have too many meetings. When do you have time to think about the customer?"

In 2018, Jeff Bezos banned the use of PowerPoint in meetings whereby rather than reading bullet points on a slide, the team sits quietly for about half an hour and reads a "six-page memo that's narratively structured with real sentences, topic sentences, verbs, and nouns." When everyone finishes reading, they discuss the topic. "It's so much better than the typical PowerPoint presentation for so many reasons," said Bezos.

On a lighter note, Spanx CEO Sara Blakely is known for being a failure driven billionaire who has no problem admitting her mistakes and allowing her employees to do the same. She schedules what she coined "oops meetings" where employees tell each other about their errors, usually turning them into funny stories. These meetings are interactive and allow the team to grow from their mistakes.

All three leaders exemplify that management by meetings is not an effective method to advance the business and move people forward. When you are closeted in meetings all day, you risk losing your grasp on your business and your people. You are trapped by your meeting agendas. You aren't walking around the halls of your organization— and that is *precisely* where you find out what's really going on. During the pandemic, it might have looked more like a quick check-in with an employee to see how they're doing. It's about checking the pulse of the people in a remote working environment. Get out of the conference room, or in this case off your screen and out of planned meetings. Have informal conversations with your people.

The calendar is a shield that keeps us from having authentic conversations and creative moments. We find ourselves having conference calls on the way to work, or in today's world before breakfast, because the meeting calendar is longer than the workday. A client I work with, said to me, (when I discussed this with her) "Rose, I have no time to think."

The other performance killer is scripted messages. If you can't explain what it is you want people to do in a simple, straightforward way, you don't understand it either. Scripted messages sent out to many people beg for a "Chocolate Conversation." You have no idea how these scripted messages will "land" for each person they reach, because you are ignoring the "Intention/Impact Loop"—without knowing how these messages are interpreted, you will not know what actions they will provoke. They may not be the actions you expected or desired and they in no way demonstrate a Leadership Conversation.

Scripted messages were introduced as a way to maintain consistency. It is okay to have 3 to 5 corporate or business goals written out for all employees so you are clear what you want people to strive for. One CEO I worked with revised the corporate goals by putting them in simple easy to understand language. One of his goals was to *"widen the revenue lead"*. Today it reads, *"Grow revenue, it's everyone's job."* This leaves little to no ambiguity—and he arrived at that simple message by having his teams work together to create a form everyone could understand. It's straight talk, and any leader can use it as a jumping off point to have an authentic conversation about what it means in your IT, Audit, HR, Legal or Finance organization.

We've discussed the fact that business today leaves us no time to gather our thoughts and have authentic conversations. As I've counseled a number of executives on this problem, we've come out repeatedly on a few key themes I think go a long way toward avoiding conversations which go nowhere:

- Keep messages simple—express them in an obvious way.
- Talk to people and do check-ins to test understanding. Be informal and helpful—no interrogations.
- Limit meetings. To determine which are necessary, ask yourself *"Where's the beef?"* Know what you need from a meeting—keep it short and crisp and move on when you reach the meeting goal.

- Carve out unstructured thought time for yourself. Google does this for all employees.
- Applications like YouTube came out of unscripted, unstructured thought time.

Don't Get Sucked In

A conversation which goes nowhere often happens when you are sucked into the *wrong* conversation. This can happen with an employee, a peer, or a boss. It's a common pitfall, so let's talk about what it is and what you can do about it.

One of my clients, Jerry, was at the time a newly appointed CEO of an agency within a publicly traded holding company. Jerry set up a meeting with the holding company's head of HR to discuss filling key positions on his team. These new appointments were part of his plan to shift the agency's focus and improve performance. He had already discussed the plan outline with the holding company's Chair and Board of Directors and they were supportive.

Meanwhile, the head of HR had reviewed the CEO's plan, but had locked onto "improve performance" instead of the appointments to the new senior team. The moment the meeting started, HR fixed on "performance" and began grilling the new CEO on performance metrics and how he planned to enforce them. The CEO tried to counter by saying he wanted to address the performance issue by filling key positions. HR thought the CEO was trying to sidestep the issue. HR said if performance was the cause for concern, then they should stay on that topic.

The next 40 minutes were spent in an uncomfortable conversation in which the CEO spent his time explaining past performance of the agency he had been appointed to lead and turn around. The HR person, who was actually a lower-ranking executive, had co-opted the conversation. Jerry initiated the meeting with one agenda, and the HR executive hijacked the conversation and took it off course.

Jerry confided in me that he didn't feel like a CEO by the end of the meeting. He could not understand how the conversation had derailed so quickly.

Well meaning, good people can easily get sucked into a conversation they never intended to have. It happens all the time. How could a conversation like this have been avoided?

I had interacted with the HR executive who was also relatively new to the holding company. He came from a traditional fortune 100 company where HR wielded a lot of power. In the holding company, HR acted more in an executive recruiter role. In agencies, talent is the product. Both executives were firmly committed to the success of their company and both were well-regarded.

Sometimes it truly does begin with a simple misunderstanding. Just as you have a desire to tell someone something, they have a desire to hear something, but they may be two different things. The CEO in the example above wanted to talk about hiring people, and the head of HR was concerned about performance. You can see how the misunderstanding occurred. This is *not* the conversation the CEO wanted to have, but he couldn't seem to redirect it.

In fact, as he tried to change course, the head of HR became even more entrenched in his point of view. Why wouldn't he let the CEO control the dialogue? The CEO had initiated the meeting—it was his to control. In this case, it seems HR felt the CEO's reluctance to have the performance conversation was concealing a hidden agenda, a desire to hide something, or a threat. The CEO's attempt to put the conversation back on course was his way of reestablishing the reason he called the meeting. Neither one of them was satisfied with the direction of the conversation, and the CEO became frustrated at his inability to steer it to what he wanted to discuss.

This was the counsel I gave the CEO. "Write the head of HR an e-mail and copy your boss, the Chairman." I told him to state his intentions:

- Be clear that you are enlisting his support in filling the key positions on your team.

- Give him a list of names you want vetted.
- Provide a deadline for when you want these positions filled.
- Let him know you are available to discuss potential candidates.
- You look forward to partnering with him to build your team.
- End of conversation.

I also advised him, "If you receive an e-mail response regarding performance, ask him to please discuss any past performance issues with the Chairman. How the agency performed prior to you coming on board is being addressed with the team but is not the primary focus. If assistance with past performances is needed, you will reach out. In the meantime, where he can really help you is getting the new talent on board. Reiterate your request to have potential candidates vetted and re-state your deadline for filling key positions." The important message to my client is that he allowed HR to co-opt his conversation.

Whenever you set up a conversation, it is your responsibility to context the topic before you jump in. In this case, when the conversation went off topic, the CEO needed to stop the conversation and clearly state he did not call the meeting to discuss past performance of the agency. The conversation had already been discussed with the Chairman and board of directors. In fact, that was why he was put in the role. He was also cleared to fill key positions, and he was there with HR to make it happen.

Reframing the Conversation

Another way to avoid being sucked into a conversation you don't want to have is to reframe it. I had that opportunity early in my career when I returned to work after the birth of my son. A woman at my office had a reputation for raining on everyone's parade. For some reason, she was put off when my co-workers began cooing over pictures of my new baby. She said, "Is that a picture of your adopted son?" I said yes, and she replied, "Well, there's nothing like having your own."

I could hear the sharp intake of breath from my colleagues in the room. They knew exactly what she meant and everyone was appalled she would come right out and say this to my face.

I know everyone expected me to say something to her—some choice words as a comeback, but I wasn't going to sink to that level. I was so enthusiastic about my baby boy, I took a moment to compose myself and said, "I know exactly what you mean. When my brother's daughter was born, I was so excited. I held my niece in my arms and felt so much love for her. I couldn't imagine having a richer experience. Now I have my own child. When I held my son—my child—there wasn't a doubt in my mind. You are absolutely right, there is no feeling that compares with holding your own child." There was a collective sigh of relief in the room. My co-worker quietly headed back to her office.

A few days later, she came into my office and apologized for what she had said. After she thought about it, she realized, for whatever reason, she was being mean-spirited. She was so surprised by my response she began thinking about her behavior. She wound up asking for my help so she could recognize the good fortune of another in no way diminished her accomplishments. She was uncomfortable—but, out of my refusal to be dragged into a conversation I was not going to have, we developed a better relationship.

Remember the conversations you decide to have are really about the conversations *you* want to have. You have the opportunity to reframe the conversation, redirect people, and take them where you want them to go.

Leadership is a conversation. Think about what it means for you as a leader to lose control of your own conversation. When you get sucked into other people's conversations, you have stopped leading. *You* are being led by *their* agenda.

Don't be afraid to remind people you're having a specific conversation about a topic you need to discuss. If they try to draw you into another conversation, they are really trying to impose their agenda on your time. Be respectful—but firm on this point. You can address their issues at an appropriate time. Continue to hold firm on what you need to discuss.

This is a world apart from leaving their concerns and needs unmet. Rather, it involves listening, forethought, and message discipline on your part. We've talked about these things separately throughout our conversation together in this book. When you don't allow yourself to get sucked in, you get your message across and you are addressing people's unmet needs. You are bringing together all the things we've talked about. You've moved from *chocolate conversations* to *leadership conversations* which can change everything about your business.

Keep in mind you have the right to be prepared for these *leadership conversations*. Use preparation to avoid being sucked into conversations you don't want to have. Better to tell someone truthfully you want to take the time to prepare a solid response to their concerns, than to divulge information you wish you hadn't, commit yourself to something you didn't intend, or answer in a way others find flippant or inappropriate. Others will accept your right to prepare if you mean it when you say it. When you have to say it, *say it*!

In the next chapter, we'll take that point even further: When you *must* say what is important to say to save your business, your company, your country, and in the most extreme cases to save lives. I really mean it when I say, "Let's *go there NOW!*"

Chapter Seven

Go There

We've all heard the expression, "Don't go there!" It crops up in movies and on TV, and, if you have kids as I do, it's a common household vernacular. I hear it all the time as I listen in on conversations: "Oh, God! What if...?" says one woman. "*Don't* even go there...!" her companion replies.

What people mean when they say, "Don't go there" is anything from, "I don't want to talk about it," to "That topic is out-of-bounds." Even when people use the phrase in a casual or joking way, they're saying the conversation has to move on to another subject—the topic is just too risky. They're warning you it's best not to discuss it, or it's something not to consider—usually because it's too scary to be true, or it's too emotional, or in business it's politically volatile to bring it out into the open.

I don't know about you, but when someone tells me *not to go there*, I'm packed and ready to do just that. When I hear that expression, I want to say, "Please don't tell me where I can't go—I'm a big girl and I can handle it!" Once I know there's an "un-discussable" out there, I must find out what it is—and why we're not supposed to be talking about it.

I'm not a fan of background conversations which never get addressed. Too often, it is those very discussions, which—if examined and defused—would open a clear space to address issues which otherwise stay unresolved. I can think of many "undiscussables" in our history that were harmful—even life-threatening—precisely because people didn't want to "go there." In business I see this often; and, without fail, it is those very background conversations that block the forward movement of the company to achieve what it wants to achieve.

Companies avoid "going there" more frequently than you would think. Topics that *can't be discussed* soon become the "800-pound gorilla" on the meeting table whenever important company policies need to be hammered out, and new directives created. This gorilla ends up blocking open initiative and new avenues of exploration. Everyone knows this gorilla is sitting there, and yet people do everything they can to avoid mentioning it.

800-pound gorilla

As an example, I worked with a publicly traded consumer products company a number of years ago where a large ownership stake was controlled by a single extended family. The gorilla on *this* company's table was executive succession. Talent and performance would only take executives so far—once they made it to the level just below the CEO's senior team, they could go no further in the company. The CEO himself was a member of the controlling family, as were a couple of the board members. The CEO was finally forced to acknowledge the issue when executives with market-making talent kept leaving the company when they'd reached a certain level. The company couldn't sustain the brain-drain.

Once I realized that executive succession—or the lack of it for everyone but the family—was *the* issue blocking vitality and growth at this company, I had some hard conversations with the CEO. I pointed out losing important talent was the cause of the company's eroding position against more innovative competitors. It prompted him to have a conversation with other members of the controlling family, and they agreed to open the issue up for discussion.

So, how did he get the gorilla *off* the table with the disenfranchised teams in the organization? He brought a large, stuffed, gorilla—about 3½ feet tall, and sat him in the middle of the table during a meeting with Business Unit senior managers.

The meeting kicked off in normal fashion, with no mention of the unusual centerpiece on the table. Incredibly, it wasn't until about halfway through the agenda before one participant, Cindy, said to the CEO, "Pat, I can't see you over this thing. Why is there a big, stuffed gorilla on the table?"

"I'm glad you asked, Cindy," the CEO said. "That represents all the stuff—like executive succession—that we really need to talk about, but never finds its way onto the agenda. It's been here so long, I figured we could just stick the gorilla there as a placeholder. We can even name it if you'd like. Of course, we can take the gorilla off the table if we talk about things like succession."

The meeting was unlike any other the executives could remember. The discussion stimulated a huge outpouring of ideas on how to tackle the problem. The story made the rounds through the company in a few short hours—and the buzz was all good. People had been thinking about this issue for years. They needed a way to get past the block, and the CEO had to be open to a new possibility for his company. The stuffed gorilla signaled that the company was ready to address and solve previously undiscussable topics.

This company now keeps a supply of small, stuffed gorillas on hand and people point to the gorilla when conversations are getting too guarded. Pulling out a gorilla and setting it on the table is the sign to honestly deal with issues instead of getting off track.

This practice is akin to saying, "Hold on, we're having a *chocolate conversation.*" I like the use of metaphors to open up conversations like this. It's a powerful, yet light-hearted, way to help you "go there."

Earlier, we talked about what people mean when they say, "Don't go there." They are letting you know you are about to trigger something that causes them anxiety, anger, or some other profound discomfort. As a leader, you may find *you* are the only one who can initiate conversations others are afraid to have, but that's exactly what having a leadership conversation looks like. Let's take a deeper look at what this means.

One of my former clients was a stickler for detail. He prided himself on being able to spot a typo in a document. He could tell the difference between an *en dash* and an *em dash* at one hundred paces. In other words, he could tell the difference between this—and this—and that became what he focused on.

I appreciate that he was telling me he had a sharp eye for detail, but he did this every time he had something to discuss; and it kept derailing conversations. These minute typos, invisible to others, undermined his confidence in the document as a whole. The content of the document—in this case, a report on due diligence preceding a $500 million acquisition—became secondary to this guy's visual trigger.

People have verbal and visual triggers. Understanding them is the first step in being able to uncover an "undiscussable" and move things forward.

For my detail-obsessed client, the focus on typographical minutia turned out to be a proxy for unease about being called out on figures. It took a while in a hard conversation with him for me to help him reach his underlying concern: He felt if his team had not properly proofed their draft before showing it to him, the *numbers* in the draft might also not be accurate. In other words, my client did not trust the accuracy of the facts and figures in the document because he saw the typos as careless mistakes and applied "carelessness" to the entire document.

This client's internal bar for accuracy was set so high he didn't want to let anything out of his hands. When my partner and I interviewed his team, they told us they were fearful about bringing anything to him in draft form as they could never get past the first typo. We suggested having an open dialogue about this issue, and they reticently agreed. They were afraid to "go there."

I asked my client if he would be willing to open the discussion between him and his team. I assured him this was the only way to solve this gridlock and get the better outcome he desired. He asked me to facilitate the two-way dialogue. I often find an objective third party can expedite the discussion and keep it on track for the solution.

When he was able to get his **concern** out into the open, the team understood why he was being so "picky." They reassured him the facts and figures in the document were well-researched and accurate. The typos were not an indication of sloppy staff work.

Once they all agreed on standards for a draft, they were able to move beyond the impasse. They created a standard that all could live with, accuracy on the facts and "roughly right" on the punctuation. This allowed his team to pull in all that could be known in a timely manner and get the information down on paper without having to sacrifice content for style. I told him, "Once you understand the substance of the content, it can be proofed and returned to you for a final edit." This guy's "roughly right" was still rigorously exact, but an agreement on a new standard allowed him to get through a draft review without being triggered, and then derailed, by minutia.

The take-away from this example is: Be *willing* to identify the triggers that get in the way, openly discuss why, and *make it okay* for you and your people to go there so all can advance the work.

Another key point is, don't lose sight of what you stand for. One of my clients early on was a manufacturing company that was eager to improve the quality of its products. They had established a series of metrics around ten different quality points. At the same time, one of the most important components of the company's reward system involved the number of units shipped within a few days of order, a number measured each month. Everyone stayed focused on that monthly "speed-to-ship" figure because it came up on reviews every quarter.

It went into "Don't go there" territory when the quality points started to become mutually exclusive with a quick "speed-to-ship" number. Sometimes, quality steps were skipped in favor of this shipping metric—but no-one wanted to walk into an Ops review and defend a lower "speed-to-ship" number because of quality. As a result, what the company stood for, "quality" started to slip.

Every manager I spoke to about a lower "speed-to-ship" number— to regain the quality levels the CEO said he was committed to, was instantly out of the conversation. The assumption the company would not tolerate this made even hearing about it taboo. In this instance, the trigger was coming from, and being reinforced by the company.

Fixing the trigger meant changing metrics in a public way so the "speed-to-ship" trigger lost its potency. I pointed out to the CEO it was important to identify what he and the company were committed to, and to get his team on board with that. It was clear he wanted *both* quality and "speed-to-ship," but the message to his employees weighed in favor of the shipping number because that's what they were rated on. By restating the importance of *both* quality standards and shipping standards, and creating review metrics for both, the CEO was able to bring the focus back in balance. Expectations on both metrics were clear and out in the open. Everyone could now get back on track.

In this case, we had to get both sides to agree to discuss something neither wanted to address. The senior team was uncomfortable about changing the metric because it meant explaining to the CEO what was going on and how he and they had inadvertently created the problem. The CEO didn't realize this was the core of the problem—he just knew quality was down and that was unacceptable to him.

This situation required what I refer to as *the artful conversation. The artful conversation* has three steps:

- It begins with *the conversation about the conversation:* This is where you create the context for what you want to address. For example, *"Larry, we want to bring something to your attention that is negatively impacting our quality standards. Without intending to, we are contributing to the problem."*

- **Get buy-in to continue:** *"Can I give you the facts?"*
- **State just the facts:** *"Our reward system compensates people for speed-to-ship. In our attempts to significantly improve this metric, the teams are achieving it at the expense of the other nine quality standards.*

At this point, if you have a solution, say so: *"We have a recommendation for resolving this issue and would like your input. Is this a good time to discuss it?"* Or simply ask for an opportunity to discuss further to resolve the issue.

It begins with the conversation about the conversation. We refer to this as the meta-conversation. Most people start with the micro, and that's why they get derailed; however, the conversation about the conversation is the meta-conversation, and this is where you create the context for what you want to address.

Remember—*leadership happens in the conversation.* Preparing for the hard conversations by creating context reduces the chances of having a *chocolate conversation* and allows you to move to a solution. You want to solve these issues early on before they become a death knell for your company.

There is an old US Army saying, "If it ain't broke, don't fix it." If you read the Second World War history from which that expression comes, you'll find it's really shorthand for, "Don't try to change what you don't have to because if you do, you may open a can of worms."

A lot of companies live by that credo. It is seductive for market leaders to look at their past success and become obsessively devoted to it. Once that happens to a leader or a company, and they lose their willingness to look at something new, the people in the company become afraid to speak up. That's when "Don't go there" becomes the order of the day. They'll follow an ill-directed leader down a path to oblivion rather than speak up and lose their jobs. We've looked at examples earlier in the book where you can lose everything by staying on an outdated course while the market is changing around you. Paying attention to what's going on out there in the world is how companies stay ahead of the relevance curve. Sometimes, to get from where you are to where you need to be, *you have to go there,* you have to take a hard look to make the difficult choices—to adjust in a changing world.

Going there often results in shaking things up. Successful market leaders like Apple do it all the time. Apple is often criticized by market analysts for introducing a new version of a product long before the previous version has shown any sign of faltering. Those analysts fear Apple leaves too much business on the table; but the truth is Apple never sees the downside of the curve. They are always one step ahead, and one new product further into the future. For Apple, their company credo is "newer, faster, better" and "watch out 'cause here we come." This keeps them consistently at the top of the curve. Additionally, Apple rewards innovation and new thinking—they are always willing to go where no one else will.

For more conservative companies, riding on past successes is easier than changing course. The people in those companies who attempt to push the envelope are few in number and often out maneuvered by those heavily vested in the status quo.

Which camp is your company in?

History bears out that it is those who "go there" which are the ones who make big differences in the world. Yes, it is always easier to stay where you are with your current way of doing things, and your current way of being. But let's look at a few who, when the world said, "Don't go there," they said, "Watch me!" and changed the world:

- Rosa Parks, a woman of color in the pre-civil rights era, refused to give up her seat on a bus to a white person. In a world of segregation and no civil rights for African-Americans, Rosa Parks "went there" by sitting silently, and changed the course of the Civil Rights movement in the United States.
- Mohandas K. Gandhi championed the cause of Indian independence by going to London to sit down with British leaders, something his colleagues found impossible to do. His non-violent stand for his country and its citizens changed the course of India.

- Winston Churchill was thwarted for years in every effort to get Parliament to listen to what was going on in Nazi Germany, and what impact that would have on the prospects for peace. He was ignored, ridiculed, and ostracized, but he kept "buggering on," From our perspective today, it's a good thing he did. He is applauded by many as having saved civilization.
- As a more modern example, Google created a competitive advantage over other sites like Bing by being the only effective search engine over the internet. They were able to reach those heights because of their size, innovation, market position, and the network effect.

If You Don't Go There, Your Customers Will

When you start to talk about the need to transform your company, you *must* have a very clear awareness of the thing that makes you, *you*. It's the unique flavor of your organization which makes you different. Some of the elements of the brand touch on it, but it's broader than that. It's what you stand for and who you are for your customers.

I've talked about Apple as a company that comes out with new products ahead of the curve. But what they really are, at their core, is a company who believes in the newest products and the newest designs—their products flow out of their core commitment to innovation and design.

What about a company like Coca-Cola? An iconic brand recognized around the globe for over a century—their mainstay being the popular "Coke" beverage which created the company and remains to this day. How do they stay ahead of the curve and continue to grow?

They had to learn the hard way that they are not simply a beverage company—they are part of the "family." A lesson their customers taught them when they lost sight of who they were to the people. They thought it was just about what was in the can.

In the 1980's, the Coca-Cola Company experienced pressure in their US markets from PepsiCo's product lines. Coca-Cola sought to get a leg up on Pepsi in 1985 by changing the iconic taste of Coke.

The "new" Coke was only on the market for 77 days[7] before a huge consumer backlash compelled the company to reinstate the old formula as "Coke Classic." Executives at Coke were inundated with letters from consumers which sounded as if a family member had died.

The public reacted so strongly to the restoration of the old formula that after only 12 weeks Coca-Cola outperformed Pepsi by year's end.

The whole event looks like a terrible misstep over what to do next, at least in hindsight. Coca-Cola executives had run focus groups on the new flavor well in advance of launch and the new product *did* score higher in blind taste tests. However, in those same focus groups, data had surfaced about the "sacred cow" nature of the Coke brand to consumers. *Why didn't they listen?*

Either they didn't know, or they forgot who they were to their customers. In the competitive rush to get in front of PepsiCo, they got caught up in the heat of the moment and believed the "new recipe" was the future for them.[1]

I want to touch on that for a moment. When the top leadership becomes committed to a new idea, known as *deal heat,* it can take on a life of its own that pushes all other considerations out of view. *Deal heat* becomes a kind of blindness—a faulty worldview which skews the judgment of leadership.

Coke executives got caught up in *deal heat* and they couldn't recognize any data which pointed to a flaw in the logic that said a new taste was needed. They would not *go there.* They were convinced they were onto the Next Big Thing. They got so carried away, no one in the organization had the courage to point out that they weren't thinking about what they meant to their customers. So, their customers had to tell them.

What they forgot is that Coke had been part of life for so many. From the time kids could drink soda pop and adults could enjoy sports events and picnics, or a simple beverage with a meal, customers counted on it as part of the family, and social landscape.

---

[7] Haoues, Rachid. *"30 years Ago Today, Coca-Cola Made Its Worst Mistake"*. 23 Apr 2015. *(https://www.cbsnews.com/news/30-years-ago-today-)*

The way Coke can—and did—grow is by watching the market for changes in consumer behavior, and adding to their product line, not changing who they are. As time went on and consumers became more fit and health conscious, Coke did come to realize their real competition wasn't PepsiCo, it was *water.* They created the Dasani brand of water to compete in that marketplace without damaging the customer loyalty for Coca-Cola.

At the end of the day, the common worldview of an organization has to be validated by market reality. You could say at one point in time that all of these worldviews once reflected a market reality:

- We provide the best travel service at the best price: Pan Am
- We provide the best user interface in business computing: Wang Labs
- Consumers know we are the best value for their photo needs: Kodak
- The Customer is King: Sears
- The firm led by Mr. Wall Street himself: Lehman Brothers
- The 28,000% growth stock: Countrywide Financial
- The business of America is General Motors: GM

Every one of these worldviews was once true—then the market reality changed and no one inside the organization had the courage to point that out. It was too dangerous to go there. Unfortunately, *not* going there, not addressing market environment changes or changes in consumer behavior, or even addressing the company's own internal change in focus, once led to the dissolution or near bankruptcy of these companies. Now, oddly enough, with the new COVID world, some of these companies, like GM and Kodak, are reinventing themselves in new ways to address the current global pandemic. GM teamed up with Ventec Life Systems under a $489.4 million dollar contract to build tens of thousands of ventilators. Additionally, Kodak Pharmaceuticals is now producing ingredients for drugs such as hydroxychloroquine.

It just goes to show, if you don't go there and address the issues, your customers will—or, they'll leave.

I saw this first-hand at Xerox. We were once a *customer-first* culture. Customers trusted us. We talked to them about what we were doing and engaged them in our new launches. Employees were encouraged to bring customer concerns out in the open. This was one of the first things we lost, and it did a lot of damage.

When we tried to change Xerox from a product company to a solutions company, we became internally focused. We stopped talking with our customers. Everyone in the company knew we were losing our way. We hadn't connected the dots from where we started to where we wanted to go. People were afraid to speak up. I remember having a conversation with a finance executive I was close to on the team. I said, "We have a lot of meetings and we produce a lot of deckware, but we don't ever talk to our customers anymore. Do they understand our message?"

She said, "I agree, Rose, but we can't go there."

Every leader needs to "go there" and initiate leadership conversations with employees and customers. It's important to do it in a way that gets things out in the open, so you get to a better outcome. This is especially important when your business is at stake. A look at the different fates of Blockbuster and Netflix shows both sides of this equation—one failed while the other went there and won their customers back.

In the video rental boom of the 1980s and 1990s, companies like Blockbuster grew explosively—it was a great niche for over ten years and Blockbuster dominated it. When consumers first started renting videos in stores, Blockbuster's huge selection ensured that even the most popular titles were always in stock. Customers grumbled about late charges—the one thing customers *didn't* like about their favorite video rental chain. Their sales were so strong and their competition so weak—let's face it, late fees were a profit-center. The company was lulled into thinking they didn't have to take the hit or deal with this one complaint.

If you don't go there, somebody else will. Netflix founder and CEO, Reed Hastings, recognized he could build a profitable DVD rental model with no expensive stores and no late fees. Blockbuster's revenues fell sharply as soon as Netflix began nationwide operations.

Like Kodak, Blockbuster scrambled to compete with the new model. Too late, and with a poorly developed version of what its competitor already had, the top executives at Blockbuster were still unwilling to address their biggest customer complaint: late fees. They still operated with the underlying assumption, "late fees won't drive customers away." Employees heard this complaint from customers time and time again. I was one of them. More than once, I asked several salespeople if late fees were a recurring complaint. One salesperson admitted to me that he and his peers regularly raised the issue with the company because so many people complained—no one listened.

Netflix was born out of what customers didn't like about Blockbuster. Customers didn't want to race back to the store to return the film. Having to pay a late fee on top of the trip added insult to injury.

As a result of the customer complaints about Blockbuster's late fees, Netflix decided to charge a low, flat subscription fee—the business model was mail order, and there were no late fees—ever. Netflix saves the overhead on stores by delivering directly to customers' mailboxes within 48 hours of a request. Customers were willing to wait a day or two to receive the movie in the mail rather than burn gas for the trip to and from the store for pick-up *and* return and *then* have to deal with the hassle of late fees.

When you reach out to your customers and uncover their concerns, as Netflix did, you can establish new standards. You will find that some things you *imagine* are deal breakers (like, "Gee, they have to wait a day or two to get their movie") are really *not* the customer standards of the moment. The standards Netflix was savvy enough to meet were *convenience* and *no late fees*.

When you understand why your competition won't "go there," you can find a winning strategy for yourself. Blockbuster assumed that *having it on hand and right away* was what customers value most. That standard had changed over the years with higher gas prices and the financial tightening most consumers were becoming sensitive to. Getting it fast and spending more in the process, was not the standard that was important anymore.

Don't make assumptions. Understand what your customers care about. Find this out by talking to them. Listen to your employees. Read blogs. Ask customers what they think. Frustration over late fees and returns was not a secret. Netflix had the conversation. Blockbuster refused to "go there." A lot of companies don't. It's a costly mistake.

Netflix was also smart enough to take advantage of Blockbuster's perceived ambivalence to the customer experience. As I said, the commotion over late fees was no secret. Neither was the fact Blockbuster seemed to be ignoring this important communication, leaving customers angry and frustrated. So, Netflix put the customer experience at the high point of their company standards.

Everyone who prefers to receive their dvd's through a Netflix account is familiar with the letters you get if anything goes wrong. Let's say a film arrives which has been damaged in shipment. You note this on the Netflix website and within an hour you'll receive a note in your email box apologizing and giving you a free rental or some other remunerative "Thank you."

Netflix will make it right with you because you are their customer and they want to remain in a relationship with you. This means taking responsibility and acting swiftly. Again, Netflix knows this is a standard and they work diligently to stay on the right side of it. They have gone on to deliver online, subscription-based services and are only offering DVDs with a special subscription. They're still listening to their customers! Other online streaming services came into play, capitalizing on the growing industry trends and advanced technologies. One example is the Amazon Fire TV (2014) and Fire TV Stick (2018) that streams Amazon Prime shows and videos. Hulu, another popular subscription video on demand service—which is majority-owned by Walt Disney Direct-to-Consumer & International, launched in 2010 as Hulu Plus, which features full seasons of television shows, providing access to new episodes. Later, in 2017, Hulu launched its Live TV service featuring linear television channels. Time Warner, now WarnerMedia, holds a stake in Hulu, and as of the first quarter of 2020, Hulu boasts 30.4 million subscribers.

Alternatively, the industry changed and new leaders figured out what consumers wanted, while keeping up with technology trends. Blockbuster turned a blind eye and eventually went bankrupt.

Be willing to "go there." Stay in the conversation with your people and your customers. Have tough conversations. Keep your worldview real and keep testing standards. That's what it takes to lead change, and that is also why it's bittersweet. You want to pick the right direction for your company, yet the cost of being wrong is steep. If you have authentic conversations with your customers and your employees, you have the foundation for transforming your business. You can try new things and make mistakes, correct them, and stay relevant in a fast-changing world.

Chapter Eight
Message Discipline

When Alan Mulally left Boeing in 2006 to join Ford Motor Company as its CEO, he faced the biggest challenge of his life. He had proven himself by turning Boeing around, and now he had an even bigger turn-around to accomplish at a beleaguered Ford Motor Company. Within two weeks of his arrival, he sent a letter to every employee in the company, outlining what he was going to do and what he expected of every employee at Ford. He told them about the business plan for the company and stated:

"Our plan will be built around three priorities:

- *PEOPLE: A skilled and motivated workforce.*
- *PRODUCTS: Detailed customer knowledge and focus.*
- *PRODUCTIVITY: A lean global enterprise."*[1]

He printed those three expectations on one side of a laminated card for all employees. On the other side was *"One Ford."*

He knew what he wanted, and he made it clear and simple for everyone.

In Mulally's drive to get Ford back on track, one of the things he did was to challenge his team to revive the company's most familiar brand. In his own words:

"I arrive here, and the first day I say, 'Let's go look at the product lineup.' And they lay it out, and I said, 'Where's the Taurus?' They said, 'Well, we killed it.' I said, 'What do you mean, you

killed it?' 'Well, we made a couple that looked like a football. They didn't sell very well, so we stopped it.' 'You stopped the Taurus?' I said. 'How many billions of dollars does it cost to build brand loyalty around a name?' 'Well, we thought it was so damaged that we named it the Five Hundred.' I said, 'Well, you've got until tomorrow to find a vehicle to put the Taurus name on because that's why I'm here. Then you have two years to make the coolest vehicle that you can possibly make.' The 2010 Taurus is arriving on the market this spring, and while it is not as startling as the original 1986 Taurus, it is still pretty cool."[2]

Could anyone mistake what he wanted after that? He sent a clear message. At the core of everything a great leader does is *message discipline*. Iconic leaders make sure they have distilled what they want to a clear, concise message that all people understand, and then they drive it through to everyone in the company. In the case of Ford, Mulally's message was simple, clear, and inspiring, something everyone in the company could line up behind.

Currently, Ajay Banga of Mastercard defines a clear message of a world beyond cash as:

1. Grow
2. Diversify
3. Build

His strategy of a world beyond cash was very simple, and another example of message discipline.

Clear the Clutter

When Steve Jobs returned to Apple, he immediately saw the brand had lost the direction he had set. The engineers were inundated with projects. The product line was all over the board, sending a confusing company message to customers. Jobs diligently streamlined the product portfolio and the direction. He simply said, *"Stop everything you are doing. We are going to make four products: two desktop computers and two portable computers, one for professional use and the other for personal use."*

Jobs told his team these computers had to be the newest and most beautifully designed. He was going to make Apple *the* computer you "had to have." To this day, people line up around blocks for Apple product launches ahead of doors opening, just to be the first to own the most forward-looking technology products on the market. As a result, the iPhone is iconic. In fact, Verizon recently launched a 5G iPhone.

Jack Welsh, the former Chairman and CEO of General Electric, told his leaders, "When you take over a business, you have three options: *"Fix it, sell it, or close it."* Again, no ambiguity; his leaders knew exactly what was expected of them. Sure, there is complexity in implementing the direction, but there is no misunderstanding about what is required. Jack passed away on March 1, 2020, and these principles still live on in G.E—much of his legacy still remains.

Legacy making leaders instinctively know the secret to running a successful business is *message discipline.* It is my *firm belief that message discipline drives operational discipline."*[8] I often tell my clients, *"People will do what's expected of them when they understand what you want them to do."*

Throughout this book, we've discussed worldviews, standards, and concerns and the role they play in how people get or miss the messages you're trying to convey. A lot of us worry that if our message sounds too simple, it may not paint an accurate picture of what it will take to make something happen. This is particularly true in a multi-billion dollar, publicly-traded corporation where leaders need to communicate with tens of thousands of employees.

Large businesses are, by nature, complex. The complexity is driven by multiple functions and departments required to deliver against objectives not always in sync across the business: The sales division has

---

[8] McMahon, Gavin. *"6 Steps To Message Discipline"*. Powerfulpoint. 22 Oct 2011. *(https://makeapowerfulpoint.wordpress.com/2011/10/22/message-discipline/)*

revenue-growth goals and finance wants the revenue, but their priority is the margin. Each department may have a different standard by which they are hearing the conversation. It is important for leaders to "speak into the listening" of each of the business functions or departments.

Going back to Ford's example, I like how Alan Mulally makes sure his message is disseminated through the ranks. He has a Business Plan Review, meeting with his direct reports every Thursday morning at 8:00 A.M. When he first arrived at Ford, there were departments, such as Human Resources, that weren't included in senior-level meetings. He changed it so the Thursday meetings included every functional discipline because, as he said, "Everybody in this place had to be involved and had to know everything."[3]

When the meeting concluded, and Mulally was sure everyone understood his message—and they each understood the others' responsibility in getting the job done, the senior managers went off to engage in their own meetings with their departments. They ensured that the message from the top was related to each of their departments in a way which made sense to them.

Once your message is clear, everything must support your message—every conversation you have, everything you do. In essence, you are branding and marketing your message with your words and your actions. In another example, let's look at a CEO of a company who acquired another business of equal size. The idea was to gain complementary product lines and access to a broader customer base. The CEO was actively trying to make a place in the new company for several of the top executives from the acquired company—retaining this talent was a key benefit of the merger.

The position of Chief Operating Officer in the new company was open. The CEO publicly said he wanted to table any discussion of who would fill the role so the combined team could focus on integrating the two companies and develop their market strategy.

A few weeks later, our well-intended CEO had a full-blown crisis on his hands. Three of his executives felt they were being tapped for the COO slot. Each conferred with one another, dropping hints they had been selected, only to find the other two felt similarly anointed.

When the CEO was confronted by each of them individually, he was bewildered. The conversation went like this. "I understand that you are interested in the COO position, but I haven't made my decision yet. You are in the running, but what gave you the impression that you had the job?" All three executives had the same response "You did!"

After talking with him about this situation, I began to connect the dots as to why he ended up with this mess. He told me he frequently rode up in the elevator with these executives. On occasion, they would chat in the elevator or on the walk to their offices. At different times, he made some encouraging remarks about the new management structure he thought were pretty neutral.

As he recalled it for me, one of these executives said to him on one of those elevator rides, "Hey did you see the financial plan I put together?" His reply was, "Yes, Mark, and you did a really good job sizing up the business opportunity we have by consolidating two of our divisions. We'll save on cost. Thanks, I like that. That's the kind of thinking I'm looking for." He remembered similar conversations with the other two, as well. He thought they were neutral, but each executive left the elevator thinking they had received a nod from him for the top slot.

When our well-intended CEO explained it was not his intention to signal the message that the COO position was decided, each one left his office feeling betrayed. One of them even resigned over the misinterpretation.

Our boy was stunned by what these executives inferred from his elevator comments. He told me, "I was just making casual conversation!" George Bernard Shaw once said, "The single biggest problem in communication is the illusion that it has taken place." Here's a principle I live by; "once you are in a leadership position, *there is no such thing as a casual conversation.* It all becomes a leadership conversation." When you lead an organization, everything you say and everything you do conveys a message—even if it's *not* the message you intended.

Communication is difficult at the best of times. It's almost impossible to get it right when you're caught off guard. People read into everything said, and they can interpret the wrong meaning.

In this case, the CEO's affable manner caused a crisis for the new company. The executive who left played a key role in the integration of the two companies. He was bitter, and his feelings were known to his direct reports and people throughout his entire organization. His leaving left a void in the company and confusion in its wake.

Bad news travels fast. The other two COO candidates became cautious and guarded. The CEO had to rebuild trust with his remaining executives, both the people in his old company and in the newly acquired company, as well.

He learned a painful lesson: *chocolate conversations can happen when you least expect them, and they can damage your credibility.* It's important to postpone conversations you are not prepared to have. If you are in an elevator or walking in a corridor and someone raises an issue or starts a dialogue, you must be careful. It's okay to say, *"This sounds important. I don't want to give you a quick response. Please get some time on my calendar and let's give this the attention it deserves."*

Death by PowerPoint

Several years ago, my partner Gavin and I were asked to sit through a cross-business unit meeting and capture the key points of several presentations. One presentation given by a senior vice president consisted of 46 slides. I didn't have a clue what this guy was talking about until he got to slide 44. We sat through 43 slides before the two big points of the presentation were shared:

- *Point One:* His division could offer a systems-integration solution to mid-volume businesses far less complex and time-consuming than the one offered by the "Big Five" system integrators.
- *Point Two:* This was a request to the audience. Members of the audience had relationships in the mid-volume accounts he and his team wanted access to. He asked to partner with them on identifying prospects from which both business units could benefit.

The following day, I asked the group if they could tell us what they heard. We got a host of different answers, none of which landed on the two big points the SVP attempted to get across.

After we listened to everyone—and realized no one heard the message, we summarized his 46-slide presentation in one sentence and the group was blown away: *"We are an alternative to big and painful system-integration efforts, and we need you to be our pitch candy.* "The room went silent for a few moments and then everyone started to laugh. Once the laughter died down, people began to see the absurdity of the presentation.

I'm not suggesting anyone making an important presentation should stand up with only two lines on a slide. What *is* true, however, is complexity leads to unclear messages and leaves people with no direction for action—which leads to an inability to execute.

What I *am* suggesting is: the point of the message must be first and as clear and as distilled as you can make it. Then, substantiate with supporting data points—in this case, the SVP could lead with: *"We are an alternative to big and painful systems integrations for midsize companies. You have access to those companies. Together we can generate revenue for both our businesses and save considerable dollars for your customers. "* Let me share how what we do works. How we can implement a simpler integration, and how our two business units could identify prospects and make calls together.

The military is the poster child for message discipline. There can be no ambiguity between orders and action. The idea is to make the line from A to B absolutely clear, no matter what mayhem is going on in the background. In fact, my partner, Gavin, trained at a military academy. He often references the way military leaders cut through debate with clear, precise instructions. If you're fighting a battle, you don't have the luxury of engaging in a long-winded, complicated speech.

General Patton is one of my favorite historical figures. During the European Campaign in WWII, his war-torn, beleaguered army asked, *"Where are we going?"* When Patten's Chief of Staff came to him with the question the soldiers wanted answered, Patten said, *"Tell them we're going to Berlin to kill those paper-hanging sons-of-bitches. "* That simple, direct message re-energized Patten's troops and they followed him into battle.

Effective military personnel, politicians, marketers, advertisers, and company leaders use message discipline to urge people to make choices or to act in a certain way. The idea is to win a battle or an election, cause customers to fall in love with your brand, or get people to execute on your strategy. Leaders and influencers need people to follow their direction. Message discipline is the basis for action.

The Importance of Listening

A critical piece of *message discipline* is listening. You have to be sure your message is landing with people the way you intended it to. If you *listen*, your people will tell you what's going on, what customers are saying, and what their colleagues are frustrated about. These are important conversations. Understanding employee and customer concerns will help you close the gap between strategy and execution. People need to *see* themselves in the picture. They want to know where the business is headed and how that impacts what they do every day.

Being intentional and inclusive when you send messages through the organization is essential. Lou Gerstner did this throughout his tenure with IBM. He wrote intentional emails that went to everyone in the company: *"Dear Colleagues, today we have acquired Lotus Notes. This acquisition is part of our strategy to provide our customers with..."* Everything anyone needed to know about *who, what, when, and how* was in his messages to the organization. This discipline was a major factor in the success of the IBM transformation. People at all levels of the organization looked forward to these communications and they paid attention to them.

You *do* have to get ideas across clearly, listen to be sure your message lands the way you want it to, and get people to act.

Politicians are masters at doing just that: Using words (sound bites) to give meaning to their ideas and then "listening" by using opinion research, focus groups, surveys, and polls to be sure their message landed with their audience in a way that moves people to action—something politicians understand well. They want people to vote for them and they can only accomplish that if voters can see themselves in what the politicians are saying. Message discipline, in this case, leads to votes.

Opinion research was, at one time only used in presidential, US senate, and gubernatorial races, but now it is common at all levels of government. Politicians at every level have learned it isn't enough to give speeches on their message; they must know how their message is perceived and if it was effective in moving voters to their side of the political aisle.[4] Often, the results of a poll or focus group will tell a politician that a theme they wanted to use just didn't fit the circumstances, and they are able to catch it in time to drop the theme or make adjustments.[5] That's what happens when message discipline is used in a conscious and deliberate way to mitigate any ambiguity, focus the message, and get people to act.

If you use *message discipline* effectively, it will translate into *operational discipline*: What you talk about and what your people focus on will determine what happens.

Let's take a look at some specific things you can do to bring message discipline to your company. As we talk about examples, keep these three points in mind: *what you say and what gets heard* equals *what gets done*:

- **WHAT YOU SAY:** Craft your message carefully—distill it to its essence. There will be detail behind these messages, but first get the main idea across; for example, Jack Welch's message, *"fix it, sell it, close it."* Be clear about what you expect and what you want people to do. Keep the language simple. Voluminous, verbose language leads to confusion. If you are communicating to a large audience with multiple functions represented, make sure your function-specific message is heard by all members of your organization, but differentiate the specifics for that role. Make it so all disciplines can see the role they play within the larger company model.

117

- **WHAT GETS HEARD:** Listen to your people. Seek feedback and do something with it. Be sensitive to what people are telling you. Understanding employee and customer concerns *closes the strategy execution gap.*
- **WHAT GETS DONE**: This is the action taken as a result of your message. Make sure that you, your leadership, and everyone accountable can see what is getting done, and that what people are doing lines up with your message.

Remember*: message discipline drives operational discipline.* Be brutally honest with yourself when you look at your results. If what is getting done is *not* aligned with the company direction, your message is not getting through to the organization. You own that! *Execution validates strategy.* Make sure *it* is clear and keep testing alignment.

It's all in the Context

Think about when you meet a group of employees. You're going to tell them something about the business and what you need them to do. They have only a small piece of the context you have. You know the whole thing. You have a lot of stuff to dump in their tiny frame of reference.

So, we have a communication gap here, creating a risk of confusion and noise. You face what my partner refers to as "the curse of knowledge." Any time you know significantly more than your audience, you run the risk of assuming they know what you are talking about. That is often not the case.

If you are the top executive, or on the executive leadership team and are in the midst of a company-wide transformation, you will know a lot more than most of the people in the company. Getting your message across to everyone requires time and preparation. At top levels of leadership, it is as important to be a *"context expert"* as it is to be a content expert. Just think of it as the difference between the forest and the trees. You're the one who can see the forest. They can only see their own tree. If you give people the back-story for how you came to the decisions and choices you've made, it helps them connect to the bigger picture. People need more context than most leaders provide.

This was a valuable lesson I learned while attending a leadership conference at MIT. I was asked to give a talk on leadership to a group of students. I was a little nervous about addressing this particular audience. Keenly aware that everyone accepted to MIT has a perfect SAT score and an off-the-charts IQ, I wondered, "What can they learn from me?"

The gentleman who asked me to speak, Dr. Kostenbaum, sensed I wasn't my usual, effervescent self. When I told him what was bothering me, he led me through a corridor into an area with an open archway. He asked me to read the inscription above the arch. It said, *"If you can put what you know into a context, it's worth 80 IQ points."*

Dr. Kostenbaum smiled at me and said, *"You, my dear, are a context expert. Do not worry. You have a lot to offer these students."* I went on to deliver my presentation and was pleasantly surprised at the warm and inquisitive reception I received from these young and brilliant students. This stuff isn't taught in most universities.

One of our clients, Martha Delehanty, handled the context challenge beautifully. She is the head of a global Human Resources team. Martha brought her team together to plan their strategy for the coming year. How did she get 100 leaders and their local teams all working consistently in the same direction? She took a look at how HR's efforts fit into the company's strategy and she did a superb job of setting the context. She boiled it all down to a few, simple goals.

This was the centerpiece of her strategy presentation: *"To transform this company, we are going to have to bring new skill sets and experience to the business. Our current talent will need to be assessed and brought up to speed. We will need to acquire new talent where we don't have the skills and experience, and we need to continue to grow leaders for the future. Here are our three strategic goals we need live by:*

- *Keep Good People*
- *Get Good People*
- *Grow good People"*

Martha detailed the specifics under each of these points. There was a lot to work out—considering there were different needs for different geographic regions. However, the basic mantra, *"keep, get, grow"* made it easy for this big group to work effectively. *How* they would make that happen and what it would look like became a story everyone was part of. A story built around a simple, clear, memorable message. Her people left the meeting with a very distinct idea of how they fit into the bigger picture, and what their leader wanted them to do.

Here is another great example. Emilio Botin, the Chairman of Banco Santander during the 2008 financial collapse, spoke about how his company stayed the course during this crisis. He had instilled three simple principles his people lived by:

"If you don't fully understand an instrument, don't buy it.

"If you will not buy for yourself a specific product, don't try to

sell it."

"If you don't know your customers very well, don't lend them any money."

His message was clear, unambiguous, and powerful. Emilio Botin knew the context in which he and his bank executives were living, and he laid out a clear path forward. Everyone in Banco Santander knew exactly what their CEO stood for and what he expected of them.

Additionally, it has long been well known that one of the secrets of effective communication is The Power of Three. People find things easier to digest when they are delivered in threes. Tie that in with the ancients' belief that less is more, and you can easily sum up clear message discipline.

Clear and Simple

In these stories, each leader did a terrific job of communicating a simple, clear direction, and staying the course. That is *message discipline* driving *operational discipline.* Let's take a closer look at how you can do this.

If everything is important then nothing is important. If everything is a priority, then nothing is a priority. Therefore, you must be ruthless in your efforts to simplify your message to its core.

This certainly does not mean dumbing your message down. We're not talking about shallow sound bites here. Every idea can be condensed to its essential meaning:

What do you want people to hear? What do you want people to do?

What do you want people to remember?

Since it's so important to take complex concepts and make them clear and simple, let me define my terms clearly and simply. *Clear* means you are distilling what you're talking about to its essence. *Simple* means using words and language an eight-year old understands.

Bill McDermott, the previous CEO of SAP, current CEO of ServiceNow, and the author of the Foreword to this book, uses the phrase, *"Keep it 'Sesame Street' simple."* That means meaningful, single-syllable words; *keep, get, grow,*—no acronyms, no complex business speak, and no corporate-speak. Just simple, clear directives that emotionally connect people to what they have to do and why.

Our *fassforward* team spends a surprising amount of time helping clients untangle the complexity they impose on themselves. They are so used to corporate-speak and things sounding complex they've become immune to it.

Cutting to the heart of the matter is always refreshing. It's not easy to do, but it's the only way to make your message heard the way you intended it to be heard.

Make it Personal

You want to say something that moves people and gets them to stop and think. Which of these would get you to sit up and take notice?

"A high closing ratio is a key factor in achieving your new business targets."

Or

"Doesn't it make you furious when you give a presentation that knocks it out of the park and your prospect STILL won't buy from you?"

Remember, you're talking to people, not machines.

A client of ours is the SVP for Customer Service in a Fortune 100 consumer goods company. She was asked to speak to a large group of customer service reps from call centers around the country. The national target for churn was .8% and the actual result was 1.0%. They were missing their churn target by two-tenths of a percent, which was a significant miss.

When she stood up to speak, the audience expected to see the usual slides with graphs showing the trends in *call in rate, first call resolution,* and *churn.* Instead, her presentation went like this:

"Yesterday 50,000 customers called into our centers around the country. 17,000 of them have been with us five years or longer. 6,800 of them decided not to renew their contract with us. That was just one day. Every thirty seconds we lose one of our customers. We need to take that personally!"

People sat up and took notice. She made it matter to them. No graphs, no corporate-speak, just an honest, simple message that made the point!

You Are Your Message

Stay strongly focused on your message. You don't need to be a celebrity CEO to have message discipline work for you. Be clear about what you're asking your people to do. Keep a razor-sharp focus on that message. Don't cloud it with filler, and don't be afraid to make it personal.

Dale Carnegie said, *"We are evaluated and classified by these four contacts: what we do, how we look, what we say, and how we say it."* Part of staying focused on your message is to remember y*ou and your message are one.* Your behaviors have to match your message. If they don't, your people will see the contrast between what you say and what you do. The result? They won't act the way you want them to. In fact, if your message is seriously out of sync with the way your people see you, you can do a lot more harm than good. Here's a perfect example:

In November of 2008, the CEOs of the Big Three U.S. automakers went to Washington, D.C. They needed massive government help to avoid bankruptcy. All three CEOs were clear and simple. Each was in sync with the other. Each made a case for urgency. they all said thousands of American jobs hung in the balance. Yet, the three CEOs were slammed and ridiculed in every major news outlet and talk show for a solid week afterward.

Why?

Each had flown to D.C. from their big, fancy headquarters on a separate, luxurious corporate jet. Think of the missed opportunity! These guys are car makers, but instead of driving their best product to Washington, they flew. And they didn't just fly—they flew like royalty—royalty begging the taxpayers for bailout money. Do you see the absurdity in the situation? The late-night talk show hosts did.

One of my clients demonstrated the what *gets said, heard and done* principle during a presentation he was making on a new go-to-market model for his teams. He's the head of one of the major offices of a media company, and his teams were doing two things simultaneously:

1. They were coming together after a large merger for the first time, and
2. They were figuring out a new collaborative model of working.

Right in the middle of his presentation, a well-respected team member stood up and said the company's commission and bonus set-up didn't take the new model into account. He said he had spoken to a finance person that very morning, and he confirmed that team members would actually lose money if they acted the way the new model urged. My client enlisted that team member right then and there to accompany him over to both the finance and legal departments to hammer out a new compensation model that complemented the new way of working. Before he left the meeting with the man he had just made his ally, he told the audience he would get back to them on changes to the comp policy—and he gave them a time-frame for when that would happen.

This is right on target. This leader had been talking about collaboration. He immediately saw the problem raised as an opportunity to model the right behavior. He suggested a way to actually solve a problem which worked for the group.

There is no more powerful way of showing a group what you're talking about than to demonstrate it in real-time in a real situation.

Everything I've said in this chapter serves one straightforward aim: *use message discipline to make things happen.* Keep in mind the connection between what you say, what gets heard, and what gets done. Make it personal. Remember, people need to connect with you and your message. Otherwise, you can't expect your people to act and do what you expect them to.

Most leaders find it difficult to be everywhere they would like to be, so they can deliver their messages the way they want. If they lead large organizations, they can't be face-to-face with all the people who follow them. They need to touch people through multiple communication mediums: webinars, e-mail, company intranets, and presentations. All these communication mediums need to connect you and your message to your people—and they to you. In our next chapter, we'll talk about how you as a leader can effectively extend your reach.

Chapter Nine

Extending Your Reach

Reaching your people on an emotional level is an indispensable part of leadership. It's the secret sauce which gets people to follow you, and—let's face it—you can't call yourself a leader if no one is following you. Some leaders have an intuitive feel for their people. Whether they are conscious of it or not, these leaders have a high emotional intelligence quotient. Others have to learn how to develop their emotional intelligence. The good news is, unlike your IQ, you can actually increase your EQ.

The first step is recognizing that leaders who have emotional intelligence get better results across the board. They are more successful at transforming their businesses and more successful at getting the best and the most from the people who work for them.

Emotional Intelligence is the ability to read people and situations. Leaders who have it know what to say and when to say it. They have the ability to kick someone in the butt when it's needed or put their arm around someone at just the right moment to restore their confidence.

There is often a misconception that leaders who have high levels of emotional intelligence are soft. To the contrary, Jack Welsh, Lou Gerstner, and Steve Jobs, all led best-in-class transformations and none of them would ever be labeled as soft.

There is also a misconception that leaders who have different worldviews, standards, and concerns cannot work easily together. One of the best examples comes from the U.S. Supreme Court and the decades-long friendship between the late Ruth Bader Ginsburg and Antonin Scalia. They could not have sat further apart on the court, but outside those walls, they often sat together at the opera and even on the back of an elephant on a trip to India. In 2015, Ginsburg said, "I disagree with most of what he said, but I loved the way he said it." In 2017 they won a Civility Award from Allegheny College based on their demonstrated friendship despite opposing political views. Their relationship and high levels of emotional intelligence both on the Supreme Court and in their private lives was an example of how we should all strive to live.

Two other leaders, in the business spectrum, who demonstrate high emotional intelligence are Jeff Bezos of Amazon and Tony Hsieh of Zappos.

Many say the foundation of Bezos's strong leadership is his high EQ. That he leads in a way which shows he's in control of his emotions and remains steady even under extreme scrutiny. In fact, recent claims challenging Amazon's workplace requirements resulted in Bezos defending his culture rather than lashing back. He spoke directly to his employees and encouraged them to reach out to him personally if they faced any issues with the HR department. This clarified his position and laid rest to the rumors, resulting in a successful leadership conversation.

Tony Shieh of Zappos demonstrates his emotional intelligence through his leadership style. He once said, "We have self-organized governance methods and meetings that happen on a regular basis, and it's all browsable and updateable online, along with, occasionally, policy updates—all of which enables any employee to contribute to the evolving structure of the organization. So, it's not so much about 'holacracy' as it is about 'self-organization.'"

Both Bezos and Hsieh have built large, strong companies while exhibiting strong emotional intelligence. Leaders with high emotional intelligence are naturals at *leadership conversations* because they know how to clear the clutter, net things out, and say things simply and directly. They don't have many *chocolate conversations*. When the occasional misunderstanding arises, they recognize it for what it is and they do something about it. These leaders know how to inspire others to align with them on their worldview, how to be specific about standards, and they are willing to face concerns head on.

The concept of emotional intelligence was first introduced to the mainstream in 1996, when Daniel Goleman authored the book, *Emotional Intelligence: Why It Can Matter More Than IQ*. The book became a popular read among many businesspeople. For those who had emotional intelligence, it gave language and validity to what previously was difficult to describe. For those who didn't have it, the book opened new territory for them to consider the concept, and to put a framework around how to develop it.

What *is* important here is that having a high level of emotional intelligence will significantly extend your professional reach. Other leaders, community influencers, competitors, and potential partners want to be in the company of a successful leader. When you pick up the phone, the people you want to reach "take the call."

My first assignment as Chief Transformation Officer at Xerox was to onboard and advise the new CIO we hired. Pat was a high-profile CIO regarded among technology gurus as a strategic change agent. She would play a key role in the transformation from the copier company to a technology solutions company. Pat was brought in to rebuild our Global IT infrastructure, define and reengineer the business core processes, upgrade and consolidate our systems, and attract new talent.

A significant aspect of her strategy was to outsource the legacy systems, hardware, and services so the new infrastructure could be funded. Included in the deal were the employees who would transition with the legacy environment. We were in the process of approving a short list of companies for the outsourcing deal when our CEO, Paul Allaire, asked that IBM be included on the final list.

After an exhaustive evaluation, the team concluded that EDS was the leading candidate and best partner for the deal.

A meeting was arranged for our CEO, Paul Allaire to meet with Les Alberthal, the CEO at EDS. Both men were awkward in the meeting. There was an obvious discomfort the two men felt with each other. Pat and our CFO tried to ease the discomfort by doing what they could to facilitate the discussion and summarize the key benefits of the deal.

A week later, Paul met with Lou Gerstner, the CEO at IBM. Paul personally met Lou in the reception area and walked with him to his office. I saw them walking and talking. Lou had his arm around Paul, laughing and chatting with him like they were old friends. Paul looked pleased with himself—like the cat who swallowed the canary.

EDS was the best option, hands down. They were willing to purchase our legacy, and they were offering a large sum of upfront money we could re-invest in the new infrastructure. IBM wasn't willing to do that. EDS had one of the best track records for managing a legacy environment. IBM didn't. In fact, people in the know at Xerox thought a deal with IBM would be like one lumbering elephant trying to tow another.

Meanwhile, Paul Allaire favored IBM from the start. Pat and the CFO met with Paul several times to extol the financial and operational benefits of EDS. Paul talked about the importance of a strategic alliance with IBM. The decision was at a stalemate. They were having a classic *chocolate conversation.*

Pat and the CFO were missing what made IBM attractive to Paul. It had nothing to do with financials and operational expertise. The attraction was Lou Gerstner. Lou was quickly becoming an internationally known celebrity CEO, while Les Alberthal was unknown outside the industry. Ironically, Les was a lot like Paul—introverted and a little stiff when you talked to him. On the other hand, Lou was animated, passionate, and a big piece of stuff—everything Paul admired and wanted to be.

Looking at this from a different angle, it was easy for me to see what was going on. I shared my perspective with my colleagues on the senior team, telling them they needed to change the conversation they were having with Paul. The talk-track I suggested went like this:

> *"Paul, we get that it would be good for Xerox to have a strategic alliance with IBM. That said, we're not sure this is the right deal around which to form that alliance. If you do the deal with Lou, he'll know he has an admirer and a fan. On the flip side, if you do the deal with EDS, you've just made the decision Lou would make—and Lou will know he has a formidable peer.*

A partnership with Lou and IBM makes sense, but not for this particular deal. You might want to talk to Lou about going to market with him in other areas of business—ones where the partnership would be focused on new opportunities for growth rather than on our past and our old stuff.

You might also consider whether you want Lou exposed to our legacy environment. It's pretty messy and fragmented and doesn't bode well for the new image we are trying to create."

That conversation won the day.

Both Pat and the CFO were intrigued by what they just heard from me. They asked me how I knew what was "really going on." I took out a sheet of paper and drew three circles:

- The first circle represented the technical sphere—*What I know.* In this sphere, people go *to* you.
- The second circle represented the social sphere—*Who I know.* In this sphere, people work with you.
- The third circle represented the political sphere—*Who knows me.* In this sphere people invest in you.

Ultimately, the technical sphere is heads down, the social sphere is heads together, and the political sphere is heads up.

I told Pat and the CFO, *"You guys were stuck in the technical sphere. You kept telling Paul what you know: the financial and operational benefits of the deal."* Paul wanted to *know* Lou Gerstner and he wanted Lou to *know him.*

It was as simple as that. Paul wanted to extend his reach by having a powerful influencer like Lou in his inner circle. He was willing to sacrifice the shorter-term financial gain for what he perceived to be a longer-term strategic gain. I told them, *"By changing the conversation, you got underneath Paul's concern and you were able to support his worldview by giving him a new standard to have a strategic relationship with Lou. This required operating in all three spheres; technical, social and political."*

We will dive deeper into the spheres later in this chapter. You will learn a simple method to apply them to any situation where you are stuck.

I've coached hundreds of senior executives in the years since and time and again, I've seen them derailed because they are on the wrong stack of mail, just as my former colleagues were. I've seen talented individuals do excellent work and yet fail to advance their ideas or their careers beyond a certain level no matter how hard they try—or how smart they are. I've also seen my share of executives—perhaps not quite as brilliant, rise and succeed to levels beyond their own and others' expectations. The executives who lost out are frustrated—they can't see why their talent goes unrecognized. What they can't see is that they are missing something vital to their success.

Let's take the COVID-19 Task Force as an example. Had Trump, who tends to be blustery and disruptive, recognized that if he had allowed Vice President Mike Pence, who by nature has a calmer and softer demeanor, to do the briefings with Dr. Fauci and Dr. Birx—and ran on his record rather than running with his mouth, people would have resonated and he would have won the day. VP Pence had the social and political sphere wrapped up while Drs. Fauci and Birx had the technical aspects. They had all three spheres covered and whether you like him or dislike him, President Trump was a disruptor. Alternatively, VP Pence could put an iron fist in a velvet glove, and that's what the country needed during the pandemic.

Why Not ME?

Take the case of a client who had a promotion opportunity in his organization a few years ago. He was an IT professional and had led a project group at a large technology company for several years. The internal CIO position had opened up and he felt he was a shoo-in for the job. He had a great reputation for getting complex projects done. He could rattle off important facts about every IT project in the company at the drop of a hat. He talked confidently with me about how I could help him once he was in the new job.

The next thing I heard, the guy was on the phone, bitterly disappointed. Someone else had gotten the promotion. The thing which hurt my client the most was the new CIO was not as technically savvy. I could hear his anguish as he said, "I am excellent at what I do. I understand what is going on in IT at this company better than anybody. But some guy who is just a suit got the promotion. How could my company do such a thing?"

My IT client had the technical sphere nailed down, but he had missed the possibility that there could be a non-technical side to qualifying for the job. The company wanted a CIO who had excellent relationships with the heads of the businesses and who could talk their language. The man they put in the job filled that bill. Technology partners were important to the company's business strategy. The new CIO had a large external network. He knew all the right people and they knew him.

There is actually a technical, social, and political component to just about every business situation. It doesn't matter if you are applying for a job or are implementing a strategy for a multi-billion-dollar company. At every level of business the technical, social, and political components are a key part of doing your job well. People who realize this and use it effectively are highly successful. People who remain blind to it are often baffled; when others move ahead of them who are less technically qualified they are left wondering why.

This was the case with my IT client. We began to work on his Emotional Intelligence using the spheres as a simple tool to expand his professional reach. Eighteen months later the CIO moved to another company and my client got the job.

You have to move beyond your comfort zone

As we develop and seek to advance our careers, we tend to rely on the area where we feel most comfortable. The way we lead, and the way others see us as leaders, reflects where we feel strongest. It's where we are the most knowledgeable, the most confident, and where we think we look best in front of others.

Our areas of greatest strength tend to fall into one of three spheres: the technical, social, or political sphere. When someone gets a promotion and we think we should have gotten it because we're perfect for the job, there is usually no mystery. It's most likely they're strong in a different sphere than we are, and that is what is making the difference in who gets the job.

Here's how the spheres play out:

People with a strong functional talent and background may feel more comfortable trying to influence others by making a technical argument. This is where they feel most competent and confident. We tend to promote them into leadership positions because they are highly skilled, knowledgeable, and experienced. They have mastered the technical sphere and the people they lead respect this. You can think of the technical sphere as ***WHAT YOU KNOW.***

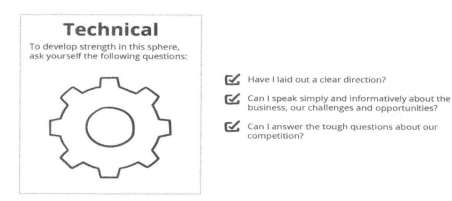

People in the technical sphere have strong subject matter expertise. They are great problem solvers. They know how to manage and get things done. They have a natural strength in managing tasks and projects end-to-end.

Some people are outstanding in the social sphere. They are excellent at bringing people together, building formal and informal networks, and relying on their relationships to influence and lead. They have technical expertise, but they are most recognized for using their social skills to make connections and secure resources outside their formal area of control. The social sphere is ***WHO YOU KNOW.***

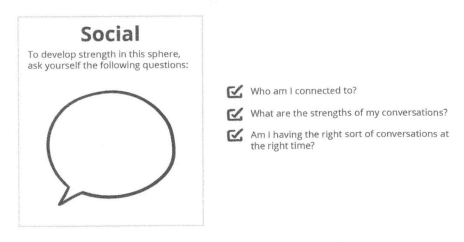

Social

To develop strength in this sphere, ask yourself the following questions:

☑ Who am I connected to?

☑ What are the strengths of my conversations?

☑ Am I having the right sort of conversations at the right time?

The leader with strength in the social sphere goes beyond the basic building blocks of courtesy and respect. They are adept at building and cultivating their influence in an informal network built on valuing relationships, being available as a resource, collaborating, and possessing strong communication skills.

Not everyone starts out with a facility for connecting with others outside of their immediate circle. One way to get started is to offer your technical expertise to others. You can lead a special task force or join one. You can share a best practice or a solution you found to a particular problem with interested parties outside your circle.

As leaders, it becomes less about doing things yourself and more about getting things done through others. Knowing how to tap into resources you need—but don't own—is a benefit of the social sphere. Becoming a well-known resource yourself is a stepping stone to the next sphere.

People who are good at balancing the different realities in the company will excel at influencing others by supporting their positions and skillfully introducing alternatives. They are known by high profile people in their company or in their larger network and are regarded by others because of it. These people use their political savvy to drive agendas and bring others around. They are operating effectively in the political sphere, which is **WHO KNOWS YOU.**

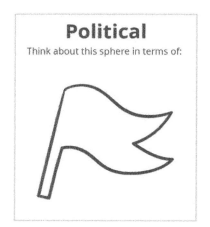

Political

Think about this sphere in terms of:

☑ Do you make others look good?

☑ Are you furthering other agendas?

☑ Have I extended my network outside of my organization, outside of my company. Am I an opinion shaper? Do I have a seat at the table?

The IT client I mentioned earlier operated almost entirely in the technical sphere. His problem was his strength didn't extend into the other two spheres, and that was impacting his career. As he went further up the career ladder, he was required to influence peers in marketing, sales, and finance. This required an ability to put what he knew into their context. This is often referred to as *socializing* an idea. My client wasn't practiced at this and was unaware that he was missing a critical skill.

He is not the only one with this dilemma. The biggest blind spot many rising executives have is recognizing their careers are about more than "what they know."

If you reflect on your career over time, the technical sphere tends to be the primary place in which we all operate early in our working lives. It is where we establish credibility in our organization and begin to develop a reputation. If we mature beyond a primary reliance on the technical sphere, our reputations will eventually translate into a professional network and broader influence, and, eventually, competency in all three spheres.

When I talk to groups about the political sphere, I ask, "Is 'political' a bad word?" Some will say "yes." Clearly, a reliance on position or connections to give you authority might make you feared in the company, but it will never earn you respect and collegiality. On the other hand, someone who can connect all the dots, understand the company, the customers, the competition, and how to put things together and make things happen is a priceless resource and a huge help to others.

The political sphere is the center of gravity of the senior leader—the Executive Leader of other executives. Leaders who are strong in the political sphere have a stature and a presence which inspires others. They have an ability to understand nuance and overcome objections. They know instinctively how to position themselves and their ideas. They understand timing—when is the best time to float an idea or bring a situation to the table. They know how to work in and around the system to get things accomplished. They manage upward beautifully and put everything they talk about in a wider context. Frequently, these are the hallmarks of a person at the apex of their career.

Each of us gravitates naturally toward one or two of the spheres, but to lead change and transform a business you have to be adept at operating in all three.

The technical sphere is where you have professional expertise and earn your credibility. We spoke earlier about this sphere's importance early on in our careers. It remains important when you reach a senior leadership position. People respect you for what you know and for "getting the job done." They need to feel confident that the one in charge knows the business and understands what's going on. Remember this sphere is about what you know. To develop strength in this sphere, ask yourself the following questions:

- Have I laid out a clear direction?
- Can I speak simply and informatively about the business, our challenges, and opportunities?
- Can I answer the tough questions about our competition?

Getting other perspectives can help supply you with useful answers. Once you have this feedback, you can assess gaps and develop a plan for communicating decisions and actions you plan to take. As you improve transparency and visibility to what's going on in the business over the course of several months, you will enhance your reputation and begin to show technical strength.

One client I worked with was promoted to president of a product division he knew very little about. He had outstanding business acumen and an amazing track record everywhere he went, but he was uncomfortable with his knowledge about the product line. He resolved to learn as much as possible in his first ninety days. I suggested he ask around about who was in the know in his organization and tap several of them as his tutors. He met with different experts in his organization on a regular basis for early morning *Coffee & Learn* sessions. These chats brought him up the curve a lot quicker than just reading hundreds of decks, product descriptions, and reports.

The social sphere concerns your professional network and the influence you have. Bear in mind "socializing" and "networking" are two very different activities (people who are not good at networking sometimes make this error). When you're good at networking, you can have a series of short, effective, business-focused conversations with any group of people. You become known for marshaling resources and getting others on board. Nurturing your network is important to you and enables you to enlist others when you need them. Remember this sphere is about both what you know and who you know.

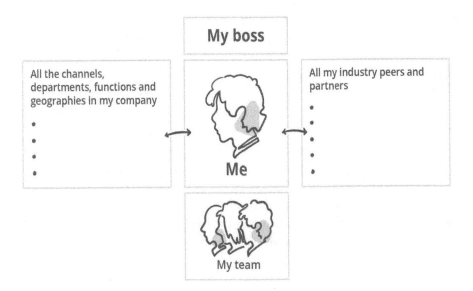

To develop strength in this sphere, ask yourself the following questions:

- Who am I connected to?
- What are the strengths of my conversations?
- Am I having the right sort of conversations at the right time?

Drawing on a simple chart may help you conceptualize this. Place yourself in the middle of a page. Put your boss, (if you're the CEO, the board is your boss) just above you and your team just below. On the right, list all of your industry peers and partners regardless of whether you personally know them well or not. On the left, list all the channels, departments, functions, and geographies in your company. What sort of relationships do you have with the leaders of these organizations and the key players on their teams? Below list the community leaders who are influencers. Building your network means being able to have meaningful conversations with people in all of these categories.

A good way to build your network is to make a point of talking with peers from other businesses and executives from the accounts you do business with. Ask them about the challenges they are facing and the opportunities they see. Offer your perspective. If you help someone else they will view you as both a resource and as someone they would like to help in the future. This builds your network and increases your ability to reach resources outside your formal span of control.

As you get good at this, people in your network will call on you for help and you won't necessarily do the work yourself—you'll refer the person to someone else you know who can help them. Your knowledge of the corporate network and its various capabilities will become valuable to others, meaning you are now showing strength in the social sphere.

The political sphere refers to your professional standing and the power you have. Getting a seat at the table allows you to influence game-changing policies and introduce alternative ideas. This is what you know, who you know, and who knows you.

Think about this sphere in terms of:

- Do you make others look good?
- Are you furthering other agendas?
- Have I extended my network outside of my organization, outside of my company? Am I an opinion shaper? Do I have a seat at the table?

Building on the chart you drew for "Building Social Strength," consider the names you placed above yours. This includes the company's leadership up to both the CEO and the Board. What other top level stakeholders are there in your organization? Do you have a parent company or venture capital investors? Are there shareholder groups or NGOs interested in your company's strategies and policies? Include all of these. Below your team, put down all the groups between you and the front line.

Since you have already plotted your peers and all the functions and geographies, you now have a diagram of exactly where you fit in the company. How are your words and actions furthering the agenda upwards, downwards, and on either side? How are you personally showing leadership in the eyes of all these groups? How are you a resource for others? How are you a champion for them? Answering these questions as you look at all the places you touch will help identify where you need to extend your professional reach.

Building strength in all three spheres will not only extend your professional reach, but it also extends your leadership reach. It is challenging for a leader to touch everyone. When you are operating in all three spheres, your credibility, network, and influence can reach a large and more diverse audience.

Many of us are unaware of the spheres—we simply play to our strengths in every situation we encounter. This is what happens when we overly rely on one sphere:

When you rely mostly on *your technical competencies*, you risk missing the political realities in your organization and you also leave necessary social networks undeveloped. People may view you as being a content expert, but someone without the ability to work the system. If people in your organization think of you as only a technical expert, they'll call on you to solve problems and love you for what you know, but it won't occur to them that you can do more. In a sense, you haven't shown them that you can. People simply won't think of you outside your area of public expertise.

You will also fall prey to missing some of the vital messages percolating in your organization. Networks do something vital—they tell you more than official channels. They give you a context for why decisions have been made, for why some things work in the company and others don't, and what is going on in the lives of the people who make up your organization. Email and formal meetings don't give you the same background information as the informal system will.

When we put too much emphasis on *cultivating social networks,* people may tend to see us as "pleasers" who won't risk relationships over difficult decisions. No company is perfect, and there are instances of people who work their networks so effectively they do get ahead—up to a point. The thing about most large companies is with each promotion, you become exponentially more visible.

In the more senior roles, you have to be able to make tough decisions or you will lose credibility with the CEO and other senior leaders. You also have to base your actions on a deep understanding of what the company does in the technical sense, or you will lose credibility with your team and with the workforce. Either way, your network will only carry you so far. You have to be a top performer and good at networking. Without the performance, people in your network will begin to feel like they are "carrying" you—and in today's environment, that situation never lasts long.

Finally, when we put too much emphasis on posturing, position and power, people see you as a "suit" and they discount your ability.

One caveat: the social and political spheres assume an ability to read situations, understand what motivates people, and communicate at a very high level. This is where both message discipline and emotional intelligence come together in the complete package to extend your reach effectively.

Let's move on in the next chapter to discuss Emotional Intelligence and how it extends your reach as a leader.

Chapter Ten

A Practical Guide to Emotional Intelligence: Here's How

A few years back, we got a call from an HR director at a large consumer products company. She wanted to talk to us about an executive named George. At the start of his career, George was one of the company's best salespeople. He outperformed everyone on his team and consistently made quota in every metric.

George went on to run a sales team and again was in the top 10% of his peers year after year. The team did exactly what George told them to do, and because he knew each of their territories as well as they did, it was hard to argue with George's direction. The company promoted George to run sales for their US Northeast region.

It was a train wreck.

As soon as we talked to George and the members of his Northeast leadership team, the problem jumped out at us. George had taken over from a very popular leader named Paula who seemed to have a magic touch with people. Everyone contrasted Paula's approachable, conversational style to George's formal, by-the-book manner. It was obvious that team members would go through a wall for Paula. They performed in spite of George, not because of him. We heard nothing but complaints about George—he was cold, he behaved as if no one could do anything right, he obsessed over plans and analysis. He couldn't simply talk with his people. Just about everything he said seemed wrong.

George knew he wasn't connecting with his people—but he didn't know why. He always got ahead by using his analytic mind. He decided to try what worked for him in the past—he called a meeting with the whole team and laid out his goals and objectives for the region, how he planned to achieve them, and what he needed from them. The team acted insulted—as if they'd been dragged to a remedial performance 101 class. George knew it didn't go as planned; but, once again, he couldn't figure out what went wrong.

We asked George what he knew about emotional intelligence. We got an extraordinary answer. "I'm not going to spend my time talking about a lot of touchy-feely, personal stuff," George said with the first real passion we'd seen. "And I'm not dragging my personal life into my job either. If that's what it takes, maybe I'm not cut out for this."

George's assumption about emotional intelligence—that it's all about "soft, sensitive, private stuff"—is very common. We've seen it before.

When you look at emotional intelligence as tapping into people and how they work, you find that it's got nothing to do with laying out your private life for all to see. You can think of yourself as a human engineer—someone with an essential business skill that drives performance. In the same way George needed to know what made his customers tick, he needed to know what would move his people.

Emotional intelligence is an indispensable part of leadership.

Some leaders have an intuitive feel for their people. Whether they are conscious of it or not, these leaders have a high emotional intelligence (EQ). Others have to learn how to develop their emotional intelligence.

The good news is that unlike your IQ, you can substantially increase your EQ. The first step is recognizing that it will transform the way you lead people and the influence you have on others. It will significantly extend your professional reach. It's worth the investment of your time and practice to become adept at operating at a high level of emotional intelligence.

There are several phrases we hear that describe people with emotional intelligence: *"He's got a good gut." "She can read the tea leaves." "He can read between the lines."* Here's a simple one we heard in one of our workshops: *"It's how you **read the gauges** and **push the buttons**."* You have to understand where people are coming from—that's reading the gauges. Pushing the buttons is knowing what to say, how to say it, and when to say it. Does it sound hard to do? For some, it comes naturally—for others, it takes practice. One piece of advice that may help: trust your gut. Don't talk yourself out of what *feels* right—yes, what *feels* right.

Reading the gauges is the first step. Think of how many times you've heard someone say, "I just don't get this guy—I can't read him." If your team is a closed book to you, perhaps you are a closed book to them.

Read Your Own Gauges

Start by getting in touch with your emotional triggers. What sets you off? How can you use your emotional triggers instead of being used by them? What triggers you is one of your own personal gauges. It's important to become aware of your triggers because they tend to stop the forward action. Here's an example:

Renee was a senior executive who liked to brainstorm with her team prior to her presentations before her board. Her personal style was to be a storyteller. She would present the facts within a rich detail of the whole picture. Then, she would send the team off to prepare the slides for her presentation. When the PowerPoint deck came back, she saw that her team had cut out all the story and reduced her natural style to a series of bullet points.

Each time this happened, Renee would become angry and upset—it triggered her to see her holistic approach summarized in a few bullet point slides. She called me to complain that her team never seemed to get the point of what she wanted.

I talked to her team and found they always left the brainstorming sessions unclear as to what she wanted, so they culled it down to its bare essence. When they brought it back to Renee, they were surprised she was angry and upset that the presentation wasn't the way she wanted it. This was a classic *chocolate conversation*.

In order to move the process forward, and to create a way Renee and her team could communicate—so Renee could receive a presentation she was proud to give to her board, I worked with Renee to uncover her trigger.

Renee realized she felt personally diminished every time her team took what she considered to be her thorough synopsis of the business and reduced it to a few bullet points—as if *she* could be reduced to a few bullet points. She wanted the board to see her as a smart businessperson, capable of relating to a context, as well as the key points she needed to get across. Once she realized what triggered her, she was able to be clear with her team about what she wanted to convey and how she wanted it illustrated in her decks. She worked with them on creating an outline and a slide-by-slide flow which would both tell her story and capture the key points. The team was relieved to finally have a handle on how to productively collaborate with her through the process and deliver what she wanted.

Renee was mature enough to look at her own trigger as her gauge. By being willing to take that on and have the conversation with her people, and work differently with them, the team was able to move the work forward together.

How people see YOU

Another gauge is how people see you. For example:

One VP in an organization we were working in was a terrible project manager who blamed his people whenever something went wrong. He often referred to them as "clueless." And, he had no idea how his people felt about working for him. Among themselves, they called him "Mr. Wonderful," which was a sarcastic code for "Mr. Disaster."

At a performance review with his boss, this executive was asked about the poor relationship between him and his team. "What are you talking about?" he asked. He was amazed at that statement. He responded, "They love me! I've heard that they even call me Mr. Wonderful!" With that, his boss realized how out of touch this executive was with his team. This was the final straw which led to his termination.

You can't afford to be clueless, but you don't need to be a mind reader, either—you just need to pay attention. Here are a few things to bear in mind:

- **Nobody likes "perfect" people.** What is worse, no one *trusts* perfect people. Someone who works at doing everything perfectly and not showing any chinks in their armor comes off as fake. It turns people off. We are all flawed—it's what it means to be human.

  People are strongly attracted to someone who is unassuming and authentic. The paradox is that authenticity creates greater regard. It makes you real. It forges a connection with people. They feel comfortable around leaders who show their muddy shoes—and they'll be a lot more likely to come to you with theirs.

- **Don't rush to fix things.** There's a big difference between being a strong leader and a "super-doer." Resist the urge to take over work you think you could do better. You're there to *guide* others—not do it for them. Your job is to set clear goals and objectives, clear the clutter and lead them through to the outcome.

- **Take other views on board.** Don't be closed to what your team has to say. Even when you have a very clear idea of what you want, talk *with* your team, not *at* them. You may be surprised by what they contribute. If you are closed to your team's input and don't actively enlist their collaboration, you may miss an opportunity. They may also take a page from your book and work the same way—closed off and "every man for himself."

- **Seek feedback.** Let other people tell you from time to time how they feel about working for you. This will give you a reading for how you come across. You don't have to do this all the time—pick the occasions that make sense. When you seek this feedback, truly listen. Don't become defensive or push your own opinion.

Read Your People's Gauges

We worked with a CEO who had been the CFO before he took over his company. To say he was a numbers guy was the understatement of the year. He sounded like a math teacher every time he pulled his senior team together—he cited facts and figures and completely turned everyone off. His slides looked like he put everything on his laptop in an Excel spreadsheet that no one could make heads or tails of.

This CEO had been successful in his career up to this point by always having the number. He found it hard to let go of what he was comfortable with even though it did nothing to move the performance of his team.

This CEO did not make it. The board recognized his financial talent but saw that he lacked the ability to convey a bigger picture and take his company forward. The greater misfortune was that this CEO left the company perplexed and unable to concede that he had caused his own demise.

The flipside of this coin is a team with which we worked that liked competing for stretch assignments. There was good-natured "one-upmanship" on the team. The leader of this team knew what they were like, and she played on their competitive nature to step up performance. It worked because she could read her people. Using this approach on every team would not necessarily produce the same result. This team leader—unlike the fired CEO—knew it's all about reading the gauges. Here are a few things to look for:

- **Different strokes for different folks.** Your team is not you. What turns you on and off may not be what turns your people on and off. You may be the type of person who likes to know what's expected and when it's needed. Once you're clear on the expectation, you'll figure out what you need to do and how to do it. Someone else may want more detail and more face time. Others like to work independently but also like being in contact with the person they work for. They enjoy the relationship, but don't need a lot of oversight.

We use a tool called "Touch/Task"[9] in our work that helps leaders get a sense of how to balance a relationship with an individual, with the work you need them to do. Reading the "how I like to interact with you" gauge is critical to making the tool work. Once leaders figure out the right balance between connecting with individuals and managing the work, they have far more effective interactions with their teams.

- **Give them what they need to succeed.** No matter what industry you're in, your team needs resources to do their job. They need tools and methods, the right level of guidance from you, and the time to do their work. In the real world, people always have to work around something that's missing—not enough information, time, or money, for example.

  Good teams can handle pressure up to a point but keep your eye on the "I'm asking too much and we have too little to work with" gauge. When the needle on this gauge moves into the red, people will start to snap at each other, complain that not everyone is pulling their weight and perhaps complain about you as well.

- **Read between the lines.** Any experienced Wall Street hand will tell you that numbers are only part of the story. Read between the lines when you evaluate the performance of your people. How do they sound when you talk to them? What body language do they use? If you need to add another project this week or up the ante, will they slide up a notch and keep humming while they get the job done, or will they burst with the added strain? You need personal contact with your people to get a sense of whether this gauge is in the red.

  Reading the gauges is vital—but it is only half the story. Armed with this information, you need to push the right buttons. Take your readings and change how your team sees you, works with you, and delivers the performance you need.

---

[9] Mazza, Frank. *"Touch/Task"*. fassforward, The How Company. 22 Feb, 2022. *(https://www.fassforward.com)*

Push the Buttons

If your company or business ran smoothly and profitably every day of the week, you'd have a lot less to worry about. You're a leader precisely because business is more complex with many more moving parts. There are multiple options and different levels of risk depending on the course you take. Your team needs direction from you.

Everyone needs to pull together toward the end goal. When you push the right buttons, you get everyone lined up behind you. This is at the core of what it means to be a leader. You deal with the conflicts, make direction clear, get commitment, and keep people focused on what's important.

- **The conflict—cooling-it-down button.** When people start to raise their voices, situations spiral rapidly out of control. This can happen in moments, face-to-face, or it can be a slow burn over days in emails. The more people lock horns, the less it is about the work.

  Press the "cool down" button by reframing the conversation. Take it out of the personal and back to the basic business problem. What unmet need got this whole thing started? Be impartial, rational, and business-focused. When tempers flare, be ready to quickly press this button.

- **The conflict—heating-it-up button.** Is there ever a time to press the "heat it up" button? Absolutely. Posing a conflict can spark creativity, innovation, healthy competition, and performance. When your team seems to be lukewarm, you want to generate some heat. Be sure you are reading your people's gauges when you press this button—otherwise, your attempt may backfire and you'll need to cool-it-down again.

- **The simple button.** If your people are locked up, overwhelmed, or don't know what to do next, press the "simple" button. Give them the three things they need to focus on. Keep the language simple and the message clear. Stop and check that everyone understands. Paint a picture for them and illustrate how they fit in that picture. People need to know what success looks like— show them. Give them a context in plain words. Make it simple so it sticks.

- **The commitment button.** Walk the talk. Behave the way you want your team to behave. Work the way you want them to work. Treat customers the way you want them to treat customers. Let others see you're totally in it with them.

  Be authentic about this—people can smell an impostor. Appreciate others in public for getting committed themselves. Use this button sparingly and for what's really important—if you go to the well on everything, your people will register a high reading on their "commitment fatigue" gauge.

- **The motivate button.** Everybody has a "motivate" button, but it's not the same for everyone. Some are motivated by money— show them how they can earn more dollars and they'll take it up a notch. Others are motivated by acknowledgment—praise their work or accomplishments and they'll go to the wall for you. Some want to know how they can advance in their career— knowing you are helping them achieve their career goals is their motivation. It is important to have a handle on what matters to each person on your team. It will serve you as a leader and positively impact the performance of the team.

- **The stepping out of the character button.** For many of us, we have a style that we are comfortable with and others are accustomed to. There are times when changing it up can be useful. Pushing the "out of character" button can change perspective, get a different reaction and often a better result.

  As a leader, you have to know what buttons to push, when to push them, and how to push them. One of our executive clients used this approach in meetings with his senior team. This guy had served a stretch in the military before his corporate career.

He spoke his mind and had a clear voice that carried. When his meetings got off track, he would lower his voice and speak in a calm, low-key manner. Once the team picked up on the changein style, the room would suddenly get quiet—you could hear a pin drop.

He knew what they expected—he had read their gauges—and he knew what buttons to press to play it differently. By speaking in a different tone and volume he stopped endless debate and got everyone focused. He was pressing both the *"cool it down"* and the *"stepping out of character"* buttons. It took only a moment, and it was effective.

For a quiet, even-keeled leader, raising your voice and acting with a bit more fire would have the same effect. The key is to know yourself, know your people, and push the right buttons.

Emotional intelligence plays a key role in our effectiveness as leaders, our influence on others and in getting high performance from our teams. We work with leaders who do it well. For them, there is nothing artificial—it's a natural part of their leadership. It's not about being soft—it's about being practical and getting the job done.

For all who have struggled with this concept—remember, this is not exclusive to one type of person. You don't have to be an extrovert or love being around people to have emotional intelligence. There are leaders who have it that are private and more introverted.

Observe people you know who have it. Watch how they read gauges and push buttons. Then take what you think would work for you and try it. Keep practicing. Tap into people on your team who have it. Where appropriate, you can ask if you're reading the gauge correctly. Remember, you don't have to be perfect; you just have to pay attention and be willing to keep at it.

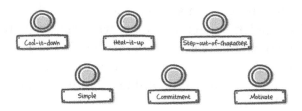

Chapter Eleven

Crisis Breeds Opportunity

I pride myself in being a *"change agent."* Yet when someone sits in my chair at the table, I immediately react by asking them to move. The truth is—I'm no different than anyone else—I like things the way they are. However, there is no growth in staying the same, there is no personal or professional development, there is no transformation. *"You're either growing or you're dying."*[10] Nothing stays the same.

We can allow change to "happen to us" or we can take on transformation and grow into a new future. This is true whether it is in our business lives or in our personal lives. If we don't actively take on change, it can come when we least expect it in the form of unexpected and often unwanted events—and most of us resist it when it comes. We all like things just as they are.

When my soon-to-be future husband and I were dating, we both had apartments on the Upper East Side of Manhattan. He lived in a one-bedroom apartment on 70th street in a walk-up building, and I lived on 72nd Street in an elevator building with a 24-hour doorman. Mine was a studio apartment.

Once we got engaged, we started making plans for where we would live together. Since he had the larger apartment, we agreed to give his place a try.

---

[10] Oppong, Thomas. *"You're Either Growing or Dying. There's No Middle Ground."* Medium. 31 Jan 2022 *(https://thomas-oppong.medium.com/youre-either-growing-or-dying)*

It was time for me to move into his apartment just as he was leaving on a business trip. He told me to make myself at home, so I did. When he left, I brought some of my things over to the apartment and started to "make myself at home."

The first thing I noticed was the uncovered M&M candies in a bowl on his coffee table. After dumping them into a plastic baggy and cleaning the bowl, I replaced them with plastic and foil wrapped Perugino soft centered hard candies. After all, doesn't everyone know you don't put unwrapped candy into a bowl and expect your guests to "dig in?"

Feeling happy with my first change, I replaced a Lucite vase he had on his dining table with a beautiful crystal vase from my apartment. Moving right along, I noticed that the paper towel was on the holder the wrong way. My mother taught me you never put your paper products on the holder where you would pull from the top. It would cause you to pull too much at one time and be wasteful. I turned the roll so you could pull the paper towel off the rack from under the roll, *as it should be.*

Once I put a few pictures from my place around the apartment and some favorite books on his shelves, I was quite pleased with the way things looked. I had made myself at home.

I went back to my apartment and collapsed in front of the TV.

Ron returned from his business trip late on a Friday night, so we decided to get together the following afternoon. When I arrived at his apartment, I noticed the crystal vase had been replaced with his Lucite one. The paper towel was back on the holder the WRONG way, and my picture frames were moved. The straw that broke this camel's back was when I discovered the M&M candies back in the bowl and my beautifully wrapped candy in the baggy on his kitchen counter. After I confronted him with, *"What happened to 'make yourself at home'?"* His response was, *"I said you could make yourself at home but that didn't mean you could **change** anything!"*

Thankfully, I had kept my apartment during our trial run.

We realized it wasn't going to work for either one of us to move into the *other's* apartment. On some deep level, we knew *changing* the *other's* space wasn't going to work—what we needed to do was to *transform* our lives together by *creating something new* that would be ours as a couple.

The third apartment gave us a new place to call our own. In chapter 4, I spoke about mergers and acquisitions being a petri dish for *chocolate conversations*. When you bring two companies together, you bring different cultures together and unique ways of doing things. Creating a new entity is important to the success of the change you are trying to make. Ultimately infusing the business with new talent, customers and solutions will only work if both entities are willing to create something new. Metaphorically it's that third apartment.

When the COVID-19 pandemic hit, many people and companies were forced into a new way of living and working. Companies were suddenly having to adapt their work environments to meet the demands of quarantines and social distancing, words that quickly became household terms. From Fortune 100's down to small and medium businesses allowed representatives to work from the safety and comfort of their homes. Restaurants became efficient at handling take-out orders and setting up outdoor seating just to survive. Never before had our country been forced to change in such ways so quickly. Many companies suffered significant losses. At the same time, other companies took off to accommodate the new standard. Notably, platforms such as Zoom and Google Meet accommodated remote meetings and conferences. COVID-19 changed America and the world in a way we'd never seen before. Amazon and other online companies have tripled their growth as a result of this crisis. Crisis breeds opportunity. Time will tell how permanent the changes are, but they certainly happened when we least expected them and they will change our lives forever. The future of work has become the hottest topic for the big consulting and research firms.

The fact is that a crisis *creates opportunity*. If you're anything like me, when something changes, you probably feel disoriented and off-kilter. It takes a while to absorb the change and craft the transformation you want to see in order to create the new life, the new opportunity, the new business. I've told you earlier in this chapter of a personal transformation I created with my husband; here is one that a friend of mine created in her professional life:

My friend, Kathy, got laid off from her company as part of a sizable restructure. She was devastated. After several tearful conversations with her, she confessed to me that she hadn't loved the atmosphere at work for some time. There had been so many rounds of lay-offs that she had been living in fear of when the next shoe would drop and her job would be gone. Her company had gone through six restructures. She fell victim to the last round.

Not too long after, she got a position with a startup. Her energy and enthusiasm for her new company and for what she was doing was infectious. Her family told her she was fun to be around again.

When we reflected on the course of events leading up to and after her layoff, she said something I will never forget, *"I got exactly what I needed. It just came in an ugly package."* My friend reinvented herself and went on to achieve greater success. The conversations you have with yourself are often the most important ones. Before you can lead anyone else, you have to lead your own life.

Leadership requires identifying the needed change, creating the new vision, and executing the vision by gaining the commitment of all members of the team. If you don't identify the change that's needed—believe me, it will be thrust upon you. Leading through change is unfamiliar territory for everyone. You're the leader—It's up to you to lead your people through it. It happens in every conversation you have. Once we accept that change is the only constant, staying the course and having the conversations necessary to keep everyone headed in the right direction is essential. Changing course when the road gets bumpy confuses people and slows down real transformation.

There is a lot of misinterpretation as to what leading a transformation really means. The best way to think about it is that you are helping people *transition from an existing form to take a new action*. While the exact way in which one business leads change may be different from how another business does it, *all* businesses must look at the following:

- What is the *climate* in which you're operating?
- What are your core assets?
- What are your barriers to success?
- What are your key differentiators? What is your competitive
- positioning?
- What are your resources and relationships?
- What are your strategic imperatives?
- What are your strategic options?
- What are your strategic shifts? What new actions do you want to take?

All of these assessments require that you have *deep, honest, raw conversations* with yourself and with your people so you can get to the heart of the profound changes you need to make to transform your business. It may mean you have to rethink your worldview and establish new standards. This gets into the most important conversations you will have.

Throughout this book, I've isolated key component parts of business transformations and their relevant case studies to create a context in which to lead the change that is critical in every business.

Epilogue

The Return to Civil Discourse

*"We're all islands shouting to each other
across seas of misunderstanding."*
— *Rudyard Kipling*

The Public Square was the physical center for discussion and debate. Imagine the Agora of Greece, the Piazza of Italy, the Meydan of Iran, the Square of England, and the village green of early America. Across the globe and across time, the public square was a vital gathering place for people to trade goods and ideas.

People gathered to take up their differences and hash them out, using the greatest tool of progress: language.

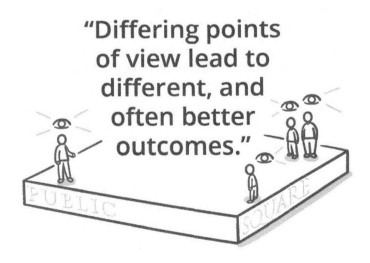

"Differing points of view lead to different, and often better outcomes."

Now the public square is virtual. It takes place on social media, in newsrooms and in business meetings over zoom.

It was once understood in think tanks, research centers and innovation labs that diversity of thought, healthy debate, and different points of view are key to achieving breakthroughs, and more often than not, better than expected outcomes. Diversity in all its forms contributes to the rich fabric of our national and global cultures.

Today we are witnessing a shutting out and shutting down of worldviews that don't align with the conventional thinking of the day.

This is happening in both the private and public sectors. People who think differently and attempt to express those thoughts are talked over, shamed and belittled. They are often referred to on college campuses and in the modern public square as outliers. People who have a different perspective are afraid to express their views or as one client refers to it; speak truth to power.

Constructive Dissent

Public squares need constructive dissent to rise above destructive dissent.

Constructive dissent is meant to share an alternative point of view, backed up by facts and supporting evidence. While it takes courage to challenge another's viewpoint, when done with the right intention, it can lead to a better outcome.

On the other hand, destructive dissent aims to ridicule, belittle, and embarrass. Knowing the difference is key to a healthy productive discourse.

CONSTRUCTIVE

Dissent, presented in a way that's helpful, not hurtful.

Backed by fact and evidence, not opinion.

Dissent that is productive, not personal.

DESTRUCTIVE

Dissent aimed to ridicule, belittle or embarrass.

Driven by narrow thinking and colored by opinion.

Dissent that is personal, not productive.

Dissent plays an important role in any organization. It is an expression of disagreement or contradictory opinions about all sorts of issues, e.g., practices, policies, people, and decisions. However, dissent can also lead to conflict, and as a result many organizations send a clear message that dissent is discouraged. According to Johny T. Garner, "there's only one problem with dissent; many people don't want to hear it, and others worry expressing dissent will cause them to be seen as negative, or it simply won't make a difference."[11]

Dissent is a driving force in organizations. Mathematician and Historian Jacob Bronowski argued that conformity kills growth, not dissent. He asked, "Has there ever been a society which has died of dissent? Several have died of conformity in our lifetime."[12]

Denny Strigl, former CEO of Verizon's wireless business, strongly encouraged constructive dissent.

Denny was often quoted as saying, "*No* is a complete sentence." These and other quotes were known in the organization as Dennyism's.

---

[11] Garner, Johny. "How to Communicate Dissent at Work." Harvard Business Review, 4 Feb. 2013.

[12] Bronowski, Jacob. Science and human values. Faber & Faber, 1956. p.79

In his book "Can You Hear Me Now" he speaks to constructive dissent as key to the success of any organization.[13]

An open work environment is one in which employees can speak their minds without fear of reprisal. This type of environment is crucial to building trust between leaders and their people. Employees are not only free to express their "real" thoughts but are encouraged to do so. They know their voices will be heard. Also, in an open environment, leaders accept "bad" news. In fact, when things go wrong, leaders will definitely want to hear about it.

There are many valuable tools to help leaders create and nurture an open work environment.

Is it your turn to talk?

In our work, we know the importance of constructive dissent.

One principle brought to light by one of our senior coaches, Jill Vander Putten, is "listening is not waiting for your time to talk."[14] Genuine dialogue can help promote better outcomes. What we often witness today is dueling monologues.

"Listening is not waiting for your time to talk."

---

[13] Strigl, Denny. "The Obligation of Constructive Dissent." Denny Strigl: Leadership Expert, Author, and Keynote Speaker, 2 Apr. 2012.

[14] This aphorism has many forms and parents, we couldn't track down the original source. It has been attributed to Simon Sinek, Ralph Waldo Emerson and Chuck Palahniuk, among others.

Businesses are seeking to find more effective and impactful ways to address their customer base and to negotiate with other companies.

A key success factor in any setting—both on the public stage and in the workplace is to address respective thoughts and concerns and identify mutually-desirable goals and resolutions.

As we watch our communities and country being torn apart from division and discord; business leaders can help. We can identify ways to set an example and encourage constructive discourse. We can help open the conversation rather than shut it down. There are well-intentioned, passionate, and compassionate people who will no longer talk to each other because they are on different sides of social and political issues. Some are afraid to speak. Others refuse to listen.

There is no conversation; there is no healthy debate

The concept of civil discourse has become as archaic as, well, the word archaic. The result is further division. We all know that a house, business, community, or nation divided cannot stand.

We as business leaders—and as communities—need to revitalize communication by and among us and come together for healthy conversation and debate.

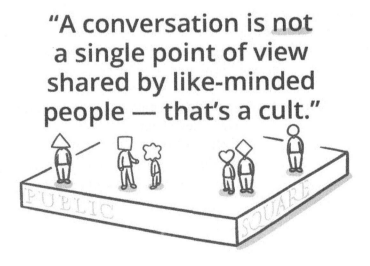

"A conversation is not a single point of view shared by like-minded people — that's a cult."

The public square exists today on social media sites such as LinkedIn, Facebook, Twitter, and others. The conversation, depending on where it lands, often only includes a single point of view shared by a group of likeminded people. You can see it on social media. These individuals reinforce each other's worldviews, set standards for themselves and others, and share the same concerns regarding people who don't agree with them.

The benefit of opposing points of view or simply a different perspective is too often ignored, shut out and not explored.

The upside to a genuine discourse is for different worldviews to be openly discussed, debated, and considered. Holding up one's side of the argument raises the level of discourse and serves to enlighten and expand thought.

Here's how

So, how do we change the conversation? It starts with you. It starts with me. It starts with each one of us. We can all listen more, talk less, and make an effort to understand different points of view.

Worldviews, Standards and Concerns

It starts with the realization that each individual over time forms a **worldview**. A worldview is simply defined by how we see the world.

Our worldview is informed by the people, places and experiences that shaped who we are and how we show up in thoughts, words, and deeds.

Our **standards** are set by our worldviews. A standard is the bar we set for ourselves and others. If we believe being on time is paramount, then people who are late will fall short of our standard. What is considered good enough by one person may be perceived by another as falling short.

When people fall short of our standards we express that by showing concern. A **concern** is simply defined as an unmet need.

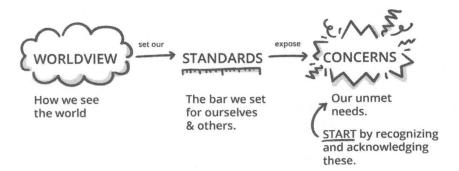

The way back to civil discourse is to start by recognizing and acknowledging the other person's concern. It's the antidote to what I call a chocolate conversation—where both parties think they are on the same page, but are not.

This is the unmet need that comes from falling short of their standard. Lastly, the other person has a worldview that informs their standard. This does not mean you have to agree with their worldview or standard. However, by understanding where the other person is coming from, you can better express why you feel differently respectfully and civilly. *You have the power to change the conversation from who's right to what's right.*

Bittersweet Change is the Best Kind of Change

We're living through this now as we move through this pandemic. Whether you're leading a company or you are the leader of your own life, recognizing that "something's gotta change" is always the first step—and that's a step of awareness. This is the beginning of the conversation for change. Remember, *Leadership happens in the Conversation*, both the conversations you have with yourself and the conversations you have with your team.

I've shown you examples from companies you've heard of, and shared stories from my experience, both personal, and in the way my team and I at *fassforward* have been able to empower our clients to grow and transform. Without fail, the impetus for change is born in that "ah-ha" moment of knowing we need to create something new.

In my experience, you can either actively seek out that moment, or you can have it thrust upon you by circumstances: you can be downsized, like my friend, Kathy, or perhaps you'll wake-up one day to realize another company has created a new business from your weakness, like Netflix created from Blockbuster's weakness—and it can be too late; OR, you can look at your business, and your life, and know change is the way to growth and expansion, and actively look for ways to progress and achieve.

I encourage you to read this book as the catalyst for the change you want to see. Don't wait for it to be thrust upon you—I say, *take it on* and be the Leader you know you can be!

Many thanks to Ajay Banga for endorsing this book! You are an amazing leader, one who made it a point to give voice to everyone you touched. Your commitment to what you referred to as the "Decency Quotient", brought civil discourse to the forefront in every conversation. How timely it is, you will now bring that to developing countries around the world, in your well-deserved appointment as President of the World Bank!

About the Author

R ose Fass is the founder and CEO of *fassforward* Consulting Group, a leading-edge business transformation boutique. Rose works with executive teams from fortune 500 companies. Her work delivers thought leadership along with methodologies, and tools that enable clients to address tough challenges, solve complex business problems, execute on their strategies and deliver bottom line results.

She has over 40 years of corporate experience in technology and consumer-based industries. During her career she has opened new businesses in the United States, been a general manager with full P&L responsibility and led major corporate transformations. As the Chief Transformation Officer at Xerox Corporation, Rose led the transition to the global industry and solutions business. She integrated acquisitions, diverse cultures, and operating units to develop and execute the new enterprise strategy. Prior to starting fassforward Consulting Group, Rose was a corporate SVP at Gartner where she was responsible for creating the new business model and working with the business units to execute on the global strategy.

A dynamic speaker, Rose is frequently invited to speak at private and public sector events. She has been a guest on CNBC, is quoted in several bestselling business books and is the author of *The Chocolate Conversation: Lead Bittersweet Change, Transform your Business*. She is listed in Forbes' 2012, Top 10 Women Business Leaders of New York. Her firm has been awarded the Inc.500/5000 for three consecutive years. Rose has a bachelor's degree from Boston University's School of Management and completed the Advanced Executive Studies Program at Harvard Business School.

Index

Dear reader, thank you for taking the time to read my book, The Leadership Conversation. Its something I don't take for granted. I hope your take aways left you feeling more vibrant, wise, and compassionate.

I wrote this book to get business people involved in the changes in our work places and in our society that we need to make. To start the conversation(s) we need to have, and follow through with them. Take action on them. Be the change we want to see.

Let's keep the conversation going. It's a privilege to receive your feedback and thoughts on this book. I would be so grateful if you could write a short review by scanning the code below.